A Promise Of Love

Fifth Printing

by
Alice Butler Bradshaw

A Promise Of Love

by
Alice Butler Bradshaw

Copyright © 1996
All Rights Reserved

PUBLISHED BY:
BRENTWOOD CHRISTIAN PRESS
4000 BEALLWOOD AVENUE
COLUMBUS, GEORGIA 31904

Also by Alice Butler Bradshaw

Poetry
Reflections
(published by Severna Park Instant Print)

Songs
He Died For You and Me
Seek and You Will Find the Master
(published by Barrett Printing)

Articles
A Tilghman Christmas
Waterman's Wife
(published by Phillip Evans Publisher)
High Adventures on the Chesapeake
(published by Broad Neck Hundred Publishers)

Cover Art By E. Lynne Kibler
Sharps Island Lighthouse, off Black Walnut Point, near Tilghman Island.

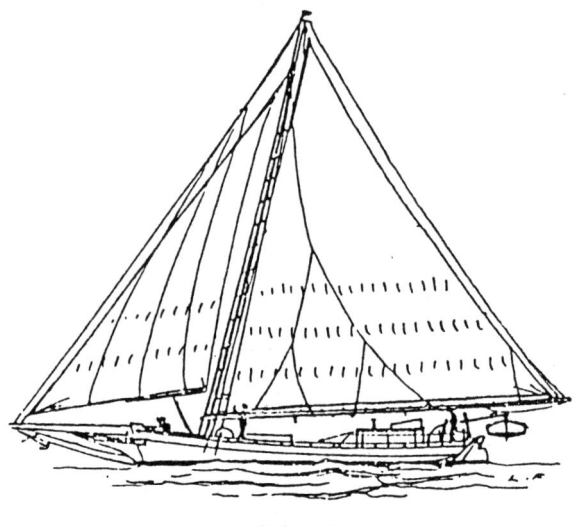

Skipjack

Dedication

This book is dedicated to my husband, Bob, who for so many years wanted me to write about our life on Tilghman Island.

Love,
Alice

Alice Butler Bradshaw

Robert L. Bradshaw

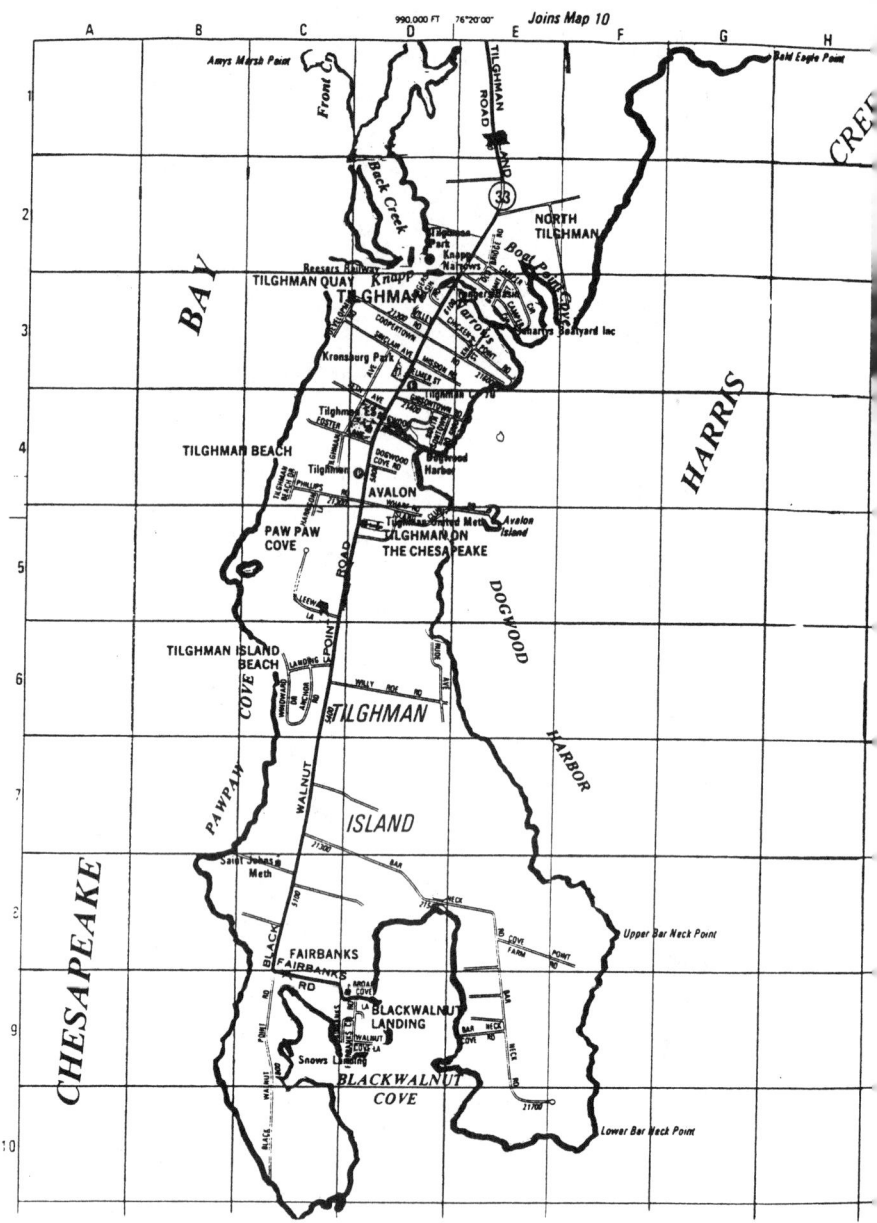

Map of Tilghman.

Introduction

"A Promise of Love" is a personal story of Alice and Robert Bradshaw's life on Tilghman Island. Located at the tip end of the Island is a small village named Fairbank. This is where Bob and Alice lived, and where the book begins.

This is the story of watermen who braved the Chesapeake Bay daily to gather from its depths treasures of oysters, crabs, fish, clams and terrapins. Food and livelihood made this band of men happy-go-lucky people. After a hard day's work of battling the high winds, dredging for oysters with ice clinging to their slickers, they congregated in Tom Faulkner's store to crack jokes, laugh and enjoy all the tall tales of the water sitting in front of the pot-bellied stove. In the summer after fishing, they would come home to a cool glass of iced tea and more fish stories at the store.

To Alice, who came to the Island in 1926, finding her Prince Charming, or as she says, her Knight in Shining Armor, a whole new world opened for her. She was always an outdoor girl, spirited in mind, and riding the Western Plains of Montana with her sisters where her family homesteaded in the 1900's. She compares her life of adventure on the Chesapeake freighting oysters with Bob, saying, "It is worse than riding a bucking bronco!"

She guides you through the ways of the Island people, a slow process of learning to love their way of life. It was a simple and loving way to live, for they are people of great faith and strong constitutions. In good times and bad, everyone shared their lives. Laughter and fun filled their homes as they made the best of what they had.

The hilarious mistakes Alice and Bob made gave them a bond like no other. Laughter was the best medicine. They found the bitter and sweet of life was the essence of love. She writes to love and remember a place now faded into the shadows of time.

The people became her family as they worked and prayed together in the Little Chapel where they worshiped. To Alice, it seemed to be a pinnacle of faith reaching out to God. For the Chesapeake bares their souls but they wouldn't have it any other way. They loved their work and their way of life.

You will find this book a history of the Watermen and their families combined with personal stories of Alice and Bob's life. She finds highs and lows with determination of working and playing together, which are precious gifts.

"The Call of the Chesapeake" is always with her.

Foreword

This book is dedicated to my husband, Robert L. Bradshaw. It was his wish that we write it together. He helped me with the first two chapters some ten years ago. We were all excited. Then somehow it was set aside for more needy projects, but I promised him the book would someday be finished.

We led a busy life. He retired from Electrolux when he was eighty, and we settled down to traveling and just having fun for once in our lives. He passed away in 1987, with the book still unfinished. My life was so shattered, the book was forgotten. Then one day I happened to look at his handwriting on the unfinished page. He had written the second chapter. In that moment, a desire to grant him his wish overwhelmed me, but memories were too sharp, the pages were covered with tears.

Five years later, I again made an attempt to grant him his wish. Time and God are great healers. I began to see life in a different way, as I believed God planned it.

I feverishly began writing day and night, picking up the memories of our life on the Island. They all came back so clearly. Every day it seemed was yesterday.

Acknowledgements

Without my family and friends, this book would not have existed. Bob was my main inspiration, wanting our children to know about our early life on the Island, and to leave them with the ideals and moral values so prevalent in our lives, and in the lives of the people of Tilghman Island.

I never learned to type, so I sat down and wrote each chapter in longhand. It was the long hours of labor for Ann Jensen, Melony Lynch, and Elviria Joy who deciphered and then typed my story on their computers.

My gratitude to D. William Comfort, D.D., President of Chesapeake Bible College and Seminar, for suggesting the publisher for me.

To Kenneth Habetler (Ken), for taking the time from his busy schedule to read my manuscript and giving his suggestions for the final draft.

To my granddaughter, Judi, and her husband, Brian, there are no words to express my thanks and gratitude for their continuous work in completing the book for publication. It was the happiest day of my life when Judi said, "Grandmother, I'll finish the book."

To God, who gave me the strength and wisdom to overcome all the trials and tribulations of a lifetime.

Thanks to one and all,
Alice

The Name of Tilghman's Island

Carry the name of Tilghman's with you,
   Tell it wherever you go
Share its glory, fellow traveler,
   Tell this story that all may know.
See the Knapps Narrows magic beauty,
   Hear the sound of Chesapeake's roar,
And the seafood bars around it,
   Fertile gold mines of the shore.
Take the sound of "Hello, stranger,
   Glad to know you, come again."
See the white sails on the Choptank,
   Sailing on the open main.
Great the blessings God has given,
   All around its fertile shores,
And the welcome that awaits you,
   Stranger, to this home of ours.
Take the beauty in its blue skies.
   Blue as any sky you'll see,
And the people, happy hearted,
   True as any folks can be.
See the color in the moonlight,
   And the set of evening sun,
Take the "Good Bye" when you're leaving,
   After all your visit's done.

By Raymond R. Sinclair
Courtesy of Lula May Sinclair Weller

The Island

As history relates, Tilghman may have been discovered by Captain John Smith in 1608. His maps were very sketchy. They showed the location of three islands which could have been Tilghman, Poplar and Sharp's Islands. Tilghman was the last name of several names given to the Island.

Many people believe that the Island was named in honor of Colonel Tench Tilghman who was aide-de-camp to General George Washington. Others believe it was named after Mathew Tilghman who owned it in 1775. Mathew Tilghman Ward, his cousin, gave it to him. A very prominent man in his day, Mr. Tilghman died leaving no heirs except for an unmarried daughter, Mary. So the property was left to his adopted son.

In 1858, the Island was laid out in plots, Upper Tilghman; Fairbank, owned by Mr. Fairbank; Bar Neck, owned by Mr. Valiant; and Black Walnut, owned by I. S. Hughes. Each of these were eventually sold to individual watermen.

Each generation passed the watermen's way of life along with the land to their sons and daughters. They were born and bred on the Chesapeake. They were, and their descendents still are, daring men of the sea. Nothing deterred them from their determination to preserve and protect their home, their way of life, and their sailing boats. Not wind, rain, sleet, or blizzard could stop them. Through the lashing waves, they brought their skipjacks and sloops safely to harbor time and time again.

It takes generations to learn the language and ways of watermen. They can be rough, tanned by the wind, yet in their own way, tender as a child to a sick or injured friend. They cared for strangers as well as neighbors. They always kept their doors open and people never passed up a meal if they visited at meal time!

Most of the families were God-fearing people from the old school of hell and brimstone. I sometimes feel that society would be better off if there were more of their kind today.

Contents

1. My First Trip to Tilghman Island 15
2. Our Courtship Years 31
3. Our Wedding 48
4. Our New Home 56
5. The Village of Fairbank 66
6. The Little Chapel and Ladies Aid 77
7. Crabbing Season and Summer Reverie 84
8. The Oyster Season 88
9. Christmas 100
10. Springtime on the Island 105
11. Our Halloween Party 113
12. My Father's Death 116
13. Our First Child 123
14. Lady Alice 126
15. Prohibition 131
16. The Great Depression 133
17. The August Storm 135
18. The Joy of a Daughter 138
19. Company from Michigan 143
20. Bob's Hairy Experience 146
21. Reed's Experience on Ice 149
22. Blue Fish Incident 152
23. Another Surprise 156
24. Trip to Norfolk 159
25. Two More Blessings 161
26. Fishing Parties 165
27. Memories 175
28. Captain Bain's Death 182
29. Leaving the Island 188
Epilogue 195
Appendix 198

1
My First Trip to Tilghman Island

For weeks, my sister Jennie had talked about Tilghman Island and how we must see the school where she taught. The children's program in the spring of 1923 at last offered the opportunity to visit the school and spend a weekend on the Island. None of us, Mother, Dad, Minibel nor I, had ever been on an Island.

Darkness had settled over Tilghman Island by the time we arrived at the school, halfway between Tilghman and the little town of Fairbank at the lower end of the Island. A faint glow of red in the sky filtered through the trees, sending fingers of crimson and gold shooting above the horizon.

Jennie hurried us out of the car. She was running late. We stepped out tentatively into the dew drenched grass. The fireflies sparkled in the darkness like a shower of diamonds, giving us a sense of wonder for this Island. The sweet fragrance of honeysuckle clung in the damp air. I stepped gingerly through the wet grass trying not to spoil my white canvas slippers.

We heard the voices of children as we pulled up to the school. They quickly clustered around Jennie as she opened the car door. For this special night, the girls wore dresses of pastel organdy, their hair in curls tied with ribbons and bows. The boys looked decidedly uncomfortable in their starched shirts, bow ties and knickers.

"Why do we have to wear these collars and ties anyway?" muttered one disgruntled young man. Jennie simply smiled. "You are a gentleman tonight," she said and patted him under his chin. "Come on now, smile, and make your parents proud."

The boy managed a bit of a grin. Jennie turned her attention to us, introducing us to our hostess for the weekend, Miss Laura Howeth.

She led us to the back of the schoolroom. We found places among the parents and friends seated in rows waiting for the program to begin. I sat on top of one of the desks so I could see better.

The curtains closed. In the hushed silence, the room was bathed in the dim glow of the coal oil lamps which provided the only light. Suddenly birds started twittering and a violin played in the background. The audience gasped with delight. The children had done a beautiful job creating a spring woodland scene with banks of flowers and greens on the stage at the front of the room. As the program began, the sun rose slowly on the horizon and the children greeted the morning with a chorus of song.

I remember very little of the rest of the program. A tall, dark-haired man standing under a light in one corner drew my attention away from the stage. He was dressed to perfection in a grey flannel suit. My heart turned somersaults.

Just that evening, I had explained to my Dad why my dress had to be ironed just right. "I might meet the man of my dreams tonight," I told him, half joking, half serious. "I could be going to my enchanted Island."

Dad laughed. "Not so fast, my lass," he said. "You have to go to teacher's college first."

His words reminded me of my plans. Like my three older sisters, I planned to be a teacher. In the 1920's, a degree meant four years of teaching and summer school combined. I had no idea at the time that this first enchanted evening would be my first step along a completely different path.

I turned to my sister, Minibel, as the first act ended. To my surprise, the dark-haired man appeared beside me. His hair was combed in a pompadour, one lock falling over the most daring, mischievous eyes I had ever seen.

"Pardon me, but I have never seen you before," said Bob Bradshaw, introducing himself with an impish grin. "You are the most beautiful girl in the world."

Blushing and embarrassed, I looked up at him and somehow managed to tell him my name. Then words just came tumbling out. I told him how Jennie had invited me and my family to the school for her students' program and that we were staying with Miss Laura Howeth over Sunday. By this time, I was gasping for breath.

His eyes held me spellbound. My mind whirled in confusion as he asked permission to walk with me back to Miss Laura's house. I had already caught a disapproving look from my father and could almost hear him telling Bob to leave his daughter alone.

To prevent that from happening, I quickly introduced Bob to my parents and Minibel. Dad didn't look very happy, but he smiled and put out his hand. "Glad to meet you, Bob," he said, then getting immediately to his main concern, "How did you meet my daughter?"

"Well Sir," said Bob, apparently not put off by my father's question, "I saw her across the room and was so afraid she would disappear, I just had to introduce myself."

"You must be a daring young man," my father responded. Bob readily agreed, and as the curtain went up again for the last act. Everyone turned their attention to the children on stage and the conclusion of their lovely program.

As everyone was leaving, Jennie joined us. She offered us a ride. Somehow, Jennie, her friend, Leslie Harrison, Minibel, Bob and I all managed to squeeze into her car. We clambered out of the car at Miss Laura's but were reluctant to pass up the beautiful June night with its full moon shining down on us.

Someone suggested we sit on the lawn, but the mosquitoes were out in force. Those who have never been on an island cannot know how intimidating mosquitoes can be. We defended ourselves as best we could by rubbing salt over our arms and legs to try to keep the pesky things at bay. There were no lotions to soothe the bites.

Before we fled inside, Bob asked me if he could take me sailing the next night, a prospect I did not relish. I had never been on a sailboat and was afraid of the water. Besides, the idea of going out at night was even less appealing.

"I'll go only if my sisters can come along," I said, hoping he would find some other activity for us. Bob hesitated and then half-heartedly agreed.

The next night, Jennie, Minibel and I walked from Miss Laura's to meet Bob at his home, which was next to the public wharf. He and Leslie were already there. We stepped into the sailboat and gaily set out. The breeze barely rippled the water, just enough to sail through the cove into the river. The glow from the moon lit our way with a silver path of phosphorous hue. To this day, I'm sure it was the most splendid night of all time.

The mosquitoes had not followed us out on the water, but they were there to meet us when we came ashore. I thought, "No more islands for me," as we said good night and walked back to the house.

Sunday morning, we went to church with Miss Laura. She played the organ at a Methodist church called the Little Chapel. I fell in love at once with the beautiful country church with high, narrow frosted windows that reached all the way to the beamed ceiling. The polished oak pews and floors gleamed and sparkled in the sunlight. In some places, the paint was peeling and the ceiling over the pulpit was frosted brown where the rain had seeped through the shingles. But although it had aged, it had a well-kept look as though each day, it was dusted, swept and polished.

That morning, the church bell seemed to speak to me especially, promising that I would return. I felt wonderfully contented, as if I belonged. After the opening song, "Oh, For a Thousand Tongues to Sing", the clear voices of the choir and congregation echoed in my ears. As I sat down, I felt again that strange warmth envelop me, like a small child being clasped in the haven of its mother's breast.

I didn't remember the Reverend Wooten's sermon because my thoughts were so jumbled. I thought of Bob and the night before, when he said goodnight and didn't ask to see me again. He knew I was leaving on Sunday, so I supposed I was just another girl in his life to be forgotten. But why did he seek me out at the school house? I was puzzled, but tried to shrug it off. When the service ended, we walked back to Miss Laura's for lunch. I squeezed Minibel's hand and whispered, "Let's walk down the road to the wharf, maybe I'll see Bob again."

"Okay, Sis, but we can't stay long. Dad wants to leave soon."

We enjoyed the peaceful stroll; tall trees lined the road with well-kept houses in between. No one was in sight to mar the beauty or serenity of the moment. Large sailboats were anchored close to the shore, and small boats were tied to posts in the harbor. The rippling waves rocked the boats gently to and fro, causing the waves to wash closer and closer on the shore.

I looked far out across the cove, shading my eyes from the glare of the sun. For a moment, I dreamed of that far-off port where the Chesapeake flowed. Mother claimed I was always a dreamer. Somehow I could see far beyond the horizon to a life of mystery.

Minibel interrupted my dreams by saying, "Look who's coming." I turned, and Bob was walking toward us. He smiled and said, "I thought you would be gone by now." I looked into his eyes. They seemed to be pleading for me to stay. But he was too shy to ask. We talked for a few minutes, then Minibel whispered, "Sis, we have to go."

Bob turned and said, "Well, I have to pump my dad's boat out."

With those words, he slipped into the rowboat that was tied to the wharf. He picked up the oars and was gone. "Good bye", I whispered.

Somehow, I hoped the wind would carry my words. I stood there stunned, hoping he would turn and wave, but no. Each lap of the oars took him farther away.

Minibel brought me back to reality. "What's wrong with you? Anyone would think you were in love."

"Don't be silly," my voice trembled, and I dashed the tears from my eyes before she could see the tears. "Bob didn't even say good bye. Why should I care? I have to go to school anyway and I don't have time for men and all those mosquitoes." I was trying hard to be brave and carefree.

Minibel smiled. "You can't fool me, Sis, I know you. It's written all over your face." She held out her hand and I gripped it.

"You always could read my thoughts," I said.

Maybe that was why we were such close sisters. All of our lives, we could depend on each other. Even after we were both married, we kept in close touch. I called her my shining angel. Minibel was always there to hold my hand when my world was falling apart. She knew just how to cheer me with jokes and laughter.

The evening was cooler now and people were out on their front porches rocking and enjoying the breeze. We had not even reached Miss Laura's when we heard Dad calling, "Come on, you slowpokes. It's time to get back to the farm."

We said our good byes to our hostess while Dad helped us into Jennie's 1920 Baby Grand Touring Car. It was the first car in our family. We loved riding in it after riding in a horse and carriage all of our lives. Jennie started the motor and we began our journey home. Dad put the top down to catch the breeze. It seemed like we traveled at a speed of one hundred miles an hour, but it turned out that we went about thirty.

Now that it was daylight, we knew why Jennie said the Island was so unique. We passed her school which was set back from the road in a thicket of tall trees. A church sat beside it with a well-kept cemetery. Old tombstones were scattered through the grounds, along with more recent ones. It looked like a peaceful, quiet place to lie beneath the sod. The rays of the setting sun rose above the sparkling blue waters of the Chesapeake beyond the cemetery. Its rays of red and gold filtered through the trees, leaving a memory never to be forgotten.

The farmlands with newly set out tomato plants stretched as far as the eye could reach. Soon the town of Tilghman appeared. On our right, a large white church, with the sign "Tilghman Methodist Church" caught our eyes. Flowers flanked the sidewalk leading to the church. Large white houses of English ancestry set back behind high hedges. It seemed we were going back in time to a colonial village, but then more modern bungalows brought us back to reality along with a school, a gas station, and several stores. A fire hall with a fire truck just pulling out stopped us and gave us a larger view of this village of about one half mile.

Jennie stopped at Knapp's Narrows Drawbridge which separated Tilghman from the mainland so we could watch the boats in the harbor. Sailboats with tall masts rocked back and forth with the breeze. We watched the bridge go up to let the boats go through, then we were on our way, leaving the village and its memories behind.

At home, my sister, Ione, waited with dinner all prepared. She taught school near Washington, D. C., and had stayed home to prepare her lessons. Ione was engaged to be married to Howard Hunt, a young man she met in New York where our family lived during the first World War.

As Ione finished putting dinner on the table, Mother told her about our visit to Tilghman. Dad went out to the stable to see how our hired man, Elmer, was doing with the evening chores. He had finished the milking and fed the cows. After looking at the rain clouds building up overhead, Elmer passed up Dad's invitation to join us for dinner, cranked up his tin Lizzie and drove off to try to reach home before the storm began.

The horses and cows were grazing peacefully in the field, unmindful of the clouds gathering in the sky. The thunder clapped and a streak of lightning flashed across the sky and Dad hurried back to the house.

Just such a storm had marked the beginning of the chain of events that brought my family to Maryland from a ranch in faraway Montana in 1916. That was the second uprooting of the family.

In 1909, when I was five, we moved west from Michigan where the long damp winters were endangering Mother's health. Mother and Dad worked hard to make our home there in the foothills of the Rocky Mountains. My sisters and I loved it there. Our horses were our constant companions and we spent hours riding the mountain trails. My sister, Susie, never went riding with us, as her health was not good. She developed rheumatic fever which resulted in a heart condition. Her heart worsened with the years. Finally in 1915 at age 16 she passed away. Mother always said she was an angel whom God sent to us for a little while.

But once more, we had to move, heeding the warning of that stormy day on a country road near our ranch.

Mother and Dad were returning home in the wagon when Dad began urging the horses ahead faster and faster. Normally a calm man, he appeared to be in a frenzy, frightening Mother as he whipped the horses into a lather. Mother had never seen him like that and before he could wreck the wagon, she took the reins and calmed the horses. Apparently a dizziness had overcome him. Dad was still in a daze when Mother drove into the yard. She took Dad's hand and smiling into his tired eyes, led him into the house.

Jennie, who opened the door, gave Mother a puzzled look. But before she could speak, Mother said, "Father needs to lie down. He is very ill. Saddle Midget and go for Dr. Brice."

We had no telephone to summon help and Jennie had to ride seven miles to town. It was two hours before she returned with the doctor. The doctor's look was grim as he told Mother that it was Dad's blood pressure that had caused the dizziness. He needed to be very quiet for a few days. Dad had never been sick before and we children were very careful not to make a sound. When the doctor returned a few days later, Dad felt better and was sitting up.

"Well, I see you are better, Frank, and your blood pressure is down." Doctor Brice kept talking as he examined Dad. "I have to tell you it is very important that you move your family to a lower altitude."

"That's impossible!" Dad was furious. "Our whole future is here. My ranch is our home. Allie and the children are happy here." Dad was nearly in tears.

Mother laid her hand on Dad's shoulder. "That's all right, dear," she said. "Wherever you and the children are, I'll be happy."

"Calm down, now, or you'll have a stroke," Dr. Brice said in a soothing manner. "Allie wants you well."

"We came to Montana for Allie's health," said Dad. "She was so sick when we first came West."

Dr. Brice looked at Mother standing nearby. Tanned from the scorching sun of the plains, her beautiful face was framed by her dark brown hair which she wore coiled in a knot at the back of her head. Her dark brown eyes looked like deep pools, shining with laughter always ready to bubble to the surface. She didn't look her forty years.

"She looks fine to me," said the doctor admiringly, "as lithe and strong as a young deer."

And so, we came to live near Oxford, Maryland, where the low altitude did wonders for Dad's health. We eventually got over our sadness at leaving our home, our friends and our horses behind.

Our new home in Maryland was really an old house, built of brick in the early 1700's and still sturdy. Nearly every room had a fireplace. A screened-in porch ran the length of the house. The kitchen reminded us of colonial days, with an enormous fireplace and hooks for iron cooking pots and kettles. We used an iron cookstove which stood at one end of the room. The table where we ate during the week was at the opposite end.

In my family, Sundays were special. Mother set the table with her best dishes. Since some of the dishes had been her mother's years ago, she prized them dearly and used them only on special occasions like birthdays and holidays. I remember one stemmed blue glass fruit dish was always placed in the center of the table with candles on either side. We still had Grandmother's white linen tablecloth, which no one but Mother was allowed to iron. In the summer, wildflowers graced the table and in the winter, a roaring fire in the fireplace lit up the room. With the candles, we needed no other light. It was lovely in the evening twilight.

But that summer's eve, on our return from Tilghman Island, we didn't linger at the end of the meal. Dad pushed his chair back from the table, "It's getting late," he said. "I think you gals had better be off to bed after the dishes are washed."

We finished the dishes and joined Mother in the parlor. Mother looked at me and said, "Alice, are you sure you feel all right? Your face is flushed."

"I'm fine," I rushed to assure her. "I just got a little too much sun standing on the wharf at Tilghman." I looked at Minibel, afraid she would say something, but instead she took my arm and said, "Let's go to bed, Sis."

"Goodnight, Mother," we joined in chorus. Dad came in. "How about a kiss for your dad, too?" He gave us a hug and a kiss. "Let's have our evening prayers and then no talking and whispering in the dark tonight." He looked sharply at me. "Do you hear me, Babe?"

From as far back as I could remember, I was "Babe" to Dad and my brother, Floyd. I was the youngest and would always be Dad's little girl.

Later when I could not sleep for all the thoughts racing through my head, I sneaked into Minibel's room, hoping to find some answers to my questions.

"I think I'm in love. I feel so light-headed. I've never felt this way before," I said. "Do you think I'm in love?"

"I don't know," Minibel answered. "I've never been there! You'd better get to bed before Dad comes upstairs."

"Mother always said we'd know when love was real," I persisted. "I'm sure I'm in love with Bob and I will love him forever even if I never see him again."

"Remember how we used to say we were going to marry a millionaire with one foot in the grave?" Minibel joked, "And then we would find a handsome young man and live happily ever after?"

"That sounds silly now," I said, feeling that this was not at all a joking matter. "If Bob doesn't come back, I'll be an old maid," I vowed.

Walking back to my room, an encouraging thought struck me. "Maybe he does love me too and was too shy to say good bye." I felt better and finally dropped off to sleep. I needed my rest, for the next day I would be on my way to Towson and a summer at the teacher's college there.

Early the following morning, Dad drove me to catch the steamboat at Easton Point. He carried my luggage on board and we stood on deck chatting for a few minutes. I wanted to tell him about Bob, but I didn't dare. He would think I was silly and that people didn't fall in love at first sight. We talked instead about my kitten, Topaz, which would be almost grown when I saw it next. When the whistle blew, I threw my arms around Dad's neck and burst out crying.

"Now, now, Babe. Summer will be over before you know it," he tried to soothe me.

"I know, Dad, take care of Topaz for me."

"Sure," he said, turning away, but not before I saw that he had tears in his eyes too. The whistle blew again and Dad walked down the gang plank. The boat's engines roared and the steamer glided away from the wharf. One more wave to Dad before the boat turned and I lost sight of him. With increasing speed the boat was steaming me on my way to Baltimore and from there to teacher's college at Towson.

Tilghman Methodist Church

Captain Bain Bradshaw

Lower Tilghman where Jennie taught school.

From left: Alice Butler and Jennie Butler.

Lower Tilghman (Fairbank School)
1919-1920 — Grades 1 through 7

Row 1: Benjamin Phillips, Neal _____, Edward Harrison, Hedge Fairbank, Theresa Bradshaw, Ida (teacher), Blanche Bozman, Calwood Somers, Roland McGarvey, Louise Gardner.
Row 2: _____ Gardner, Myrtle Bradshaw, Jenette Cummings, Louise _____, _____ Gardner, Chester Kapisak, _____ Gardner, Reynolds Larrimore, Meba Fairbanks, Russell Phillips.
Row 3: Eva Phillips, Mildred Bradshaw, Kenny Phillips, Monie Jenkins, Edward Phillips, Harry Fairbanks, Clifford Bozman, Gilbert _____.

Courtesy of Carroll Wesley Newcomb

The Bradshaw Home

Mary Bradshaw, Josephine, Theresa, and Beatrice.

2
Our Courtship Years

This was my first trip to Baltimore by myself. Mother declared that it was time I grew up and learned the way of the world by striking out and being part of it.

I arrived in the city in the middle of the afternoon. The tall buildings loomed bigger than I had ever seen before. I felt like a tiny dot in the midst of all the traffic. Everyone seemed to be in a hurry to get somewhere. I heard street cars clanging and occasionally a horse and cart with vegetables and fruit meandered through the noisy maze.

Mother had instructed me to wait for a street car with the Baltimore & Ohio Railroad sign on the front. Several cars passed, and I noticed how the people got on. I wanted to cross the street, but how could I manage with so much traffic? I waited a few minutes. The blazing sun beat down and I longed to be home, sitting under the cool shade of the trees. When I saw the car I wanted, I darted across the street and nearly fell when one of my heels caught in the cement.

"Steady, lady, don't be in such a hurry," said a man, catching my arm to steady me. "I don't know why women wear those high heels anyway." At that moment, I wondered the same thing.

"I have to catch that street car, Sir," I gasped.

"That's all right. You'll make it," he said. Helping me on the car, he tipped his hat and watched as I dropped my nickel in the slot and found a seat. I felt everyone's eyes looking at me and my clumsy ways. When the car reached the train station, I picked up my suitcase and with all the dignity I had, I proudly walked into the station and bought my ticket to Towson.

I felt so lonely all by myself. To my surprise, when I turned from the ticket window I saw Mary Clough from my high school class. I called her name excitedly! When she saw me, we hugged like long lost friends. We discovered that we were both on our way to summer school. We chatted on the train, trying to reassure each other that everything would be all right.

At Towson, Mary and I gathered our suitcases and stepped off the train into a tiny wayside waiting room. Glancing around, we saw a group of large buildings in the distance at the top of a long hill. Lifting our suitcases, assuming we had to traipse up the hill, we began the long walk. Hot and exhausted, we reached the top.

We stepped through the door of the first building we came to, and said "Thank you, Lord!" in unison. Above our heads we saw a sign reading "Register." We signed in and received our keys. Yet another surprise awaited us: we were to be roommates! A lady directed us to our room, and flopping on our beds, we thought about getting out of our traveling clothes, and taking a shower when a bell rang.

"Dinner in fifteen minutes!" said a girl sticking her head in the door. "You'd better be in line."

Mary and I hurriedly jumped in the shower and changed into cool, clean clothes. The bell rang again and we joined the line in the dining room for our first meal at summer school. It wasn't Mother's cooking, but we ate hungrily. We consoled ourselves that maybe it would improve as time went on.

We soon made friends, learned the routine, and I settled down to study. It seemed we walked miles each day from building to building and up and down stairs. I wondered how some of the heavier girls remained so heavy!

I was so tired that I slept soundly, but Bob's face kept appearing in my dreams. He seemed to be telling me something. He left me so abruptly, I thought everything was over between us. I tried to blot him out of my mind, but to no avail. His daredevil eyes and mischievous grin kept me awake. Men! Who needed them anyway? I couldn't be bothered; I tried my best to concentrate fully on learning to be a teacher.

Then one Sunday, the dean informed me that I had an unexpected visitor in the sitting room. I was stunned to see Bob. No letter. No phone call. There sat the same old spontaneous Bob, shyly awaiting his fate. I was overwhelmed just seeing him again! Inwardly, I shook like a leaf, I was so excited. I couldn't manage to speak at all!

"Will you forgive me?" he asked, before I said a word. "Is there a private place where we can talk?"

I led him outside and we sat under the trees. He apologized for parting so suddenly the last time when he left me standing on the wharf without an explanation.

"I couldn't trust myself to say good-bye," he said. "Can we start over again?"

I agreed tentatively. Soon he asked me for a date, the first of many weekend dates we would have.

One Sunday, we took the steamboat to Tolchester, a booming summer resort at that time. Unfortunately, we got back after the ten o'clock curfew and met with locked doors. Luckily, one of my friends stood guard and let me in after Bob knocked nervously. I didn't have a second to spare getting to my room. The dean could have come walking through the halls at any moment. Without a goodnight to Bob, I flew upstairs. No more late nights, I told myself. We watched the clock more carefully. We managed a few quick trips to the Hippodrome Theatre in Baltimore to see stage shows and movies.

Our dates ended shortly before the school term ended. Bob's father needed help repairing and painting his boat for the fall oyster dredging. Bob was crabbing, the watermen's summer living. We exchanged letters, but didn't see each other again until school was out and I returned home.

Back at home, Minibel kept company with Roland Sommers, from the Island. He and Bob came in Roland's boat on weekends. The four of us enjoyed swimming together in the Chesapeake Bay, unpolluted at that time. Nothing serious had developed between Bob and me.

In the fall, a private school in Easton offered Minibel a teaching job. I was appointed to a country school near Vienna, Maryland. Minibel knew I dreaded the mosquitoes which were supposedly more bothersome in Vienna than on Tilghman. She asked Mr. Boston, the school superintendent, if we could exchange schools. He told her that he didn't like mosquitoes either! So I taught at the private school, while Minibel took the country school. Maybe it was her destiny. She eventually met her future husband there.

The Christmas holidays came. Bob and I exchanged gifts: he gave me a wrist watch and I gave him my picture. The watermen were in the midst of the oyster dredging season, and Bob was running oysters. That left no time for dates.

On March 3, 1923, Jennie and Leslie were married. My older sister, Ione, married her New York friend, Howard Hunt, the same month. They moved to New York, but Jennie continued to teach and live on the Island.

Minibel and I both attended summer school that summer. I came home for the Fourth of July to visit Jennie and see Bob at the same time. As I stood on her lawn, I heard a car drive up with Bob at the wheel. I thought he would stop, but he sped past in a flurry of dust. Then, with a sudden squeal of brakes, he turned the car and screeched to a halt in front of me.

"How about a ride?" he asked innocently.

"Ride with you, after you went flying past like that? No, thank you!" I replied indignantly. I turned on my heel and walked into the house.

"Have it your way, but you'll be sorry," I heard him say with a laugh as he drove away.

That night, I went to the movies with Jennie and Leslie. and who should we see but Bob. I rethought my earlier tantrum and was ready to make up. Apparently Bob wasn't ready. He completely ignored me. That night, I cried myself to sleep. I knew in my heart that I had no one to blame but myself. I consoled myself by thinking, "Men! Who wanted them anyway?"

Later, Bob wrote that he was only teasing me and asked me to forgive him a second time. I guess when you're in love, love wins out. I took the blame and we were on speaking terms again.

In the fall of 1924, I accepted a position to teach disabled children in Langhorne, Pennsylvania. I felt unhappy venturing so far away, but I truly believed teaching was my destiny. I came to love this beautiful place in the country with acres of trees and walking paths through the woods. I taught year-round because the children lived at the school. Bob and I saw each other only on holidays. Bob had never told me that he loved me, but I sensed it in his words and manner. I soon discovered the truth in the old adage, "Absence makes the heart grow fonder."

Summer arrived. Who should appear on my doorstep but the same old spontaneous, daring Bob. As usual, not a word by phone call or letter.

"Why are you here," I asked. "Did the crabs stop biting?"

"I have a job building a bridge over in Norristown," said Bob, who had traveled many miles by train to see me.

"You're pretty sure of me, aren't you?" I said.

"Sure I'm sure," he replied confidently. "I'm going to marry you."

"Who said so? You haven't asked me yet."

"Well, I am, one of these days when I make enough money. You wait and see."

I wasn't convinced. "I have two more years of school," I reminded him. "You'll forget me by that time."

"Please don't say no, honey," he pleaded. "I love you."

What could I say to that earnest plea? Bob stayed in a small hotel in the village on Saturdays and Sundays. From that day until the bridge was finished, he left his waterman's trade behind and worked as a carpenter, which served him well in years to come.

We happily spent all our spare time getting to know each other. We took long, peaceful walks along trails to a rushing brook and wandered through the quiet woods. Sometimes children from the school walked with us. I waded in the brook with them, but Bob watched from the bank. He claimed it was too tame when you'd known the dashing waves and windblown white caps of the Chesapeake.

Nestled among the trees, we discovered a springhouse with a bubbling spring falling in cascades of rushing water. On hot days, we sat on a bench inside. The cool dampness refreshed our bodies from the searing heat of the sun. I often think of the springhouse now when I am troubled. It brings me peace to imagine Bob's comforting arm around me in our special place.

We sat together on high stools at the town drug store not far away and talked as we drank gingerale and ate crunchy pretzels. Sometimes, we took a group of children on a small passenger bus to a ferry. It took us to a summer resort where we enjoyed picnic lunches from the school. Under the restful shade of the trees, we admired the bathing beauties on the beach.

Bob told me stories of his life at home and how he loved the Chesapeake. "That's the only life I've ever known," he said. With pride, he told me that his dad was a great sailor and taught him to sail when he was fourteen. "One day, I'll take you out in a storm. You'll love standing at the helm with the wind blowing in your face and the spray covering your body." I shivered and drew closer to him. I could feel the dashing waves against my body. "Please honey, no storms for me thank you," I said. "I'll take the Bay when it's calm and beautiful."

"You're just a cream puff, afraid of everything," he chided.

"I am not," I said, reminding Bob that I was as much at home on the back of a horse as he was on a boat. "I'll just bet *you* can't ride a bucking bronco."

"I'm not even going to try," he said and put his arm around me to steady me as we walked back from the beach over the rough stones.

At night, we sat out on the school grounds, watching the stars and listening to the sharp whistle of the train running behind the school. The world seemed to be a fairyland of peace and tranquility and we were totally in love.

Our good times together ended abruptly when the bridge was finished. Bob returned to Maryland and his old trade. I asked to leave the school because I felt so lonely after he left. Another teacher replaced me within two weeks. Suddenly, I was bidding everyone goodbye. I found it hard to leave because the children and I had become so close. They gave me small handmade gifts which touched my heart. I knew I'd never forget them and my experience at the school. With mixed feelings, I headed for Maryland.

Bob met me at the station and took me home. We were overjoyed to be together again! I finished out the summer at home and hoped for another school in the fall.

Minibel came home heartbroken because she and Roland had a misunderstanding. Their engagement had been called off. I tried to cheer her up, taking her along with Bob and me when we went out, but to no avail. I suggested that he wasn't worth her tears, but in my heart, I knew how I would feel.

One day, Bob suggested a trip to Sharp's Island, off Black Walnut Point on Tilghman Island. I asked Minibel to join us, but she preferred to stay behind and go horseback riding. I joined Bob aboard the boat, and we set off with Bob at the helm. As I sat at the bow, I peered down and saw a crab crawling on the floor of the boat. Knowing nothing about crabs, I reached down to pick it up. The next thing I knew, it pinched my fingers firmly and painfully in its claws. I screamed and startled Bob so much that he almost fell overboard. I began slinging my hand vigorously in all directions trying to shake off the crab. He yelled, "Don't shake your hand!" By the time he reached me, I managed to fling the crab off, and my finger dripped blood.

"Don't you know you never try to throw a crab? They just bite harder," he said, bandaging my bleeding finger with his handkerchief. "Honey, if you weren't hurting so badly, I would laugh," he said. "Now remember not to pick up a crab again unless it's dead."

"I won't, don't you worry," I assured him, "and don't you laugh at me. I'm not a waterman like you."

Our journey took us to the lighthouse. Bob pointed to a small piece of land rising from the water nearby, which was all that remained of Sharp's Island. He explained that at one time Sharp's Island was connected to Tilghman. It had a steamboat landing and a hotel that people flocked to for summer vacations.

I found it hard to imagine that the harsh pounding of the waves had washed most of Sharp's Island into the Bay. I couldn't believe what I saw had once been an island big enough for a hotel or anything else. "I visited a lot when I was a boy," Bob said, "but I never saw the hotel because it had been gone for years."

"In the 1800's," he continued, "there were 700 acres where people farmed. Believe it or not," he winked, "there was even a legend of Blackbeard the Pirate."

"Oh my!" I gasped, "tell me!"

"It's pretty bloody; are you sure you want to hear it?" he asked.

"It's only a legend, so go ahead, I'm game," I said, and moved closer to him, expecting another Treasure Island tale. Bob put his arm around me and commenced the story.

"Blackbeard anchored his ship on the East side of Sharp's Island. He heard of a prize-laden rich treasure ship that was scheduled to run down the Bay. He waited patiently for his prey. He was so intent on making his plans that he failed to see the schooner "Harlowe" lying inside the cove which was not far from his vessel.

The Schooner's Captain, Joshua Covey, recognized the pirate ship. He decided that this was a match for Blackbeard. Joshua took a couple of his crew, crawled into a yawl boat and silently rowed over to Blackbeard's ship with his sword in his teeth, pirate fashion he managed to climb aboard without being seen."

"Oooh!" I exclaimed, grabbing Bob's arm.

"I told you so," Bob grinned. "In the meantime, Blackbeard was leaning over the rail looking up the Bay for the first sight of the treasure ship. Quickly, Joshua crept up behind Blackbeard and with one swipe of his sword, he cut off the pirate's head, which went tumbling into the water."

By this time, I was expecting a bloody head to be popping around the boat, but I was intent on the rest of the story so Bob kept on.

"When this unexpected event happened, Blackbeard's headless body rose from the deck, picked up a copper plate which was inscribed with the location of all his treasure caches. The plate sank into the Bay. Blackbeard's headless body jumped into the water and swam three times around the ship, then disappeared from view forever."

I was about ready to drop down in the bottom of the boat, shutting my eyes tight to keep out the vision which swam around our motor boat.

"That's not all, honey", he kept on holding me tight, "that isn't all the legend. It doesn't say what fate held for Captain Covey's small crew or the words which were inscribed on the copper plate. Those who wish to believe should look for the copper plate by first encountering a man eating herring. Honey, why don't we start looking for the copper plate and be rich!"

I shivered and kept my eyes in the boat. "No, thank you, when I go looking for treasure it will be on land, not at the bottom of the Bay!" I replied hastily.

I was glad we were close to the lighthouse. Bob yelled to the keeper who was standing out on deck watching us approach. He had tended the lighthouse for many years and knew Bob as a frequent visitor. Bob stopped the motor, pulled the boat alongside the rope ladder up to the deck and tied up. The wind tossed the boat back and forth, pulling it against the mooring rope. As I hung on to the side of the boat and watched the swaying ladder, I decided that I was definitely safer in the boat than on the ladder.

After much coaxing and coaching, Bob encouraged me to try the ladder. "I'll be right behind you," he reassured me as I put my foot on the first rung. "Just look up, not down, and you'll be all right."

After hearing the legend, it was best I had to look up or I would have envisioned Blackbeard's headless body still floating in the water. I gritted my teeth, did just as he said, and made it to the deck above. Once there, I felt glad I'd made the effort and overcome my fear. There was so much to see!

The two lighthouse keepers were confined to a small space, but they had furnished it with all of the comforts of home. We climbed a winding staircase up to the second deck where they kept the lamps, their brass polished until it shone like gold. We clambered up another flight of stairs to the upper deck and marveled at the view outside. The great, expansive Chesapeake spread out before us. I think I fell in love with the Bay at that moment, but it was a love tempered with fear. When I looked down into the mighty waves pounding the foot of the lighthouse, I became frightened. I felt like a tiny helpless speck. My stomach turned somersaults and my love for the Bay faded.

"Let's go back," I said with a shaky voice. Bob didn't argue and we quickly returned to the first deck. I wanted to put my feet on solid ground once more. Bob suddenly grabbed me in his arms and lifted my face to his.

"Will you marry me?" he said.

"What?" I asked, completely unnerved.

"Marry me."

With no time to sort out my feelings, I felt ready to do anything to get back in the boat.

"Yes," I said, unhesitatingly. It happened quickly, but I never regretted my answer. The electric spark that brought us together never lost its light.

My wayward thoughts returned to the present. I still faced the problem of getting from the lighthouse to the boat. It proved worse climbing down. Bob forged ahead, reminding me again not to look down, "Just shut your eyes and feel for the ladder with your feet."

Bob calmly climbed down the wildly swaying ladder. I would have felt safer on a bucking horse, knowing I'd land on firm ground if I fell off. I could picture myself being swept off to drown in the Bay if I fell off the ladder.

"Now that wasn't so bad," exclaimed Bob, once we were safely back in the boat and on our way again. "At least we're engaged."

"I think you planned this so I would say 'yes' before I thought, or be thrown overboard. Besides, you have to ask my dad. Maybe he'll say 'no.'"

"In that case, I'll carry you away and elope," said Bob daringly.

Darkness had nearly come when we reached our dock at home. We saw Dad in the kitchen washing for supper as we walked up the steps to the back door. With a wink and a 'wish me luck' grin, Bob whispered, "I might as well get it over with."

I sat down on the steps to wait, not knowing what Dad would say. Both he and my mother wanted me to finish college. I held my breath.

Momentarily, Bob came out beaming. "Well hon, as of this moment, we are officially engaged."

Dad came out and hugged me close. "I want only the best for you both," he said, "but remember young man, if you ever mistreat my girl, you'll have to deal with me." As I looked at Bob towering over my father, I almost had to laugh, but I knew Dad meant every word he said.

A week later, Bob presented me with an engagement ring: a beautiful diamond in a silver filigree and sapphire setting. As he slipped it onto my finger, the shiny gems reflected light from the coal oil lamp in a perfect rainbow. I thought it was the most beautiful ring in the world and looked up to kiss him.

"Remember dear," he said, "This is for keeps. I love you now and forever."

But fate put one more hurdle between us and the altar, perhaps to teach us both more patience.

My parents and I moved to a farm in Federalsburg, a small country town among many on the Eastern Shore, with large shade trees lining the streets. You knew by the Victorian houses it must have been settled in the 1800's. It wasn't much of a business town. Probably Nobel's Lumber Mill was one of the largest mills in the area. Large stone churches also gave you an impression of English architecture.

Our farm was three miles into the country. The house was large like our home in Oxford. The sitting room and dining room both had the characteristics of age. The finely carved wood mantles over the fireplace kept the rooms cozy and warm.

Dad told Bob he could help cut the wood if he was going to court me and keep the fires burning. Bob gladly accepted this, he and my dad had a great relationship.

All of the walls and doorways were in need of paint. I was the only girl home so it fell to me to paint, putty and hold the wallpaper for Dad to hang.

Mother wanted everything to be in order for I decided this would be a lovely place for our wedding. The picture is still vivid. The long stairway leading into the parlor reminded me of old southern estates with winding stairs with walnut polished rails.

Dad and Mother were happy here in this home, which they intended to be the last home they would buy. Here Dad grew a large peach orchard and acres of cantaloupes. On a beautiful spring morning the following May, I awaited a call from Bob. When the call never came, I found that a whole day stretched ahead of me with nothing to do. I looked around to see the spectacular blooms of the arbutus. I admired God's creative, delicate design, remembering how my sisters and I rode horseback up the mountain trails in Montana and how the beautiful shooting star flowers covered the ground just like the arbutus did.

Without another thought, I headed to the stable to go riding. As usual, I chose a path through the woods, stopping now and then to enjoy the chorus of birds echoing through the air. I loved nature. For as long as I can remember, I enjoyed watching the beauty of the world outside. I felt glad to be marrying a man who shared my love of the outdoors. We looked forward to living in the country, even though we wouldn't have a farm. I would still enjoy dramatic sunrises, restful sunsets, and a nighttime sky filled with glittering stars.

That spring day, I drank in the beauty in everything I saw. If only it could be like this forever, I wished silently. I didn't realize how soon my feeling of peace would evaporate.

On my way home, I met Russell Bradley, a neighbor, out riding. We rode the rest of the way together and arrived in our yard to find Bob waiting there, unexpected as usual. I began to introduce Russell, but Bob would hear none of it. He'd jumped to the conclusion that I was cheating on him and flew into a rage.

"If you prefer him to me, go ahead and spend the day riding with him," he thundered.

"If that's all the faith you have in me, I won't bother to explain! I'll go riding whenever I want," I said angrily. "Take your ring and go home to your mosquitoes!"

Without another word, Bob jumped in his car and left, and I burst into tears. Mother rushed out to see what had happened. I explained about Bob's jealousy when he thought I'd been riding all day with Russell.

"He'll be back," Mother said, putting her arms around me. "If he loves you and he's the right man for you, the Lord will find a way to bring him back."

"But I gave him back my ring and told him to leave," I sobbed.

"Temper, temper," said Mother, leading me into the house. "When will you two ever learn?"

Mother was right. Bob appeared the next week. No phone call. Just a knock on the door. I looked a mess, sitting on the floor in a pair of old overalls painting a chair.

"May I come in?" he asked sheepishly.

"Sure you can come in," I said, trying to ignore him and continuing to paint. I saw the misery in his eyes and wondered how I could be so cruel, but reminded myself that he had been cruel too. I still didn't know what was best to do, so I kept painting, not trusting myself to speak.

"Please, honey, take the ring back," he said, pulling me to my feet. "I'll get down on my knees if it will help. I said the ring was for keeps and I meant it."

I could see the love in his eyes and suddenly knew what to do. I held out my hand. "I'm sorry too," I said. "Please forgive me."

He took my hand, put my ring back on my finger, and it never came off again. We set the date for our wedding: June 5, 1926. We learned many lessons the hard way, but throughout our marriage, we never forgot that first important lesson. As I look back to those first years, I realize that if we hadn't had faith in God and in each other, our lives together would have been lost.

If My Heart Could Sing

If my heart could sing
The echo from above
Would ring throughout eternity
The fathom of my love.
If my heart could speak
The words would ever be
You are my one and only love
This darling can't you see.
If we could walk together
With love our guiding star
We'd find new worlds to conquer
No matter where we are.
If my heart could whisper
Through the stillness of the night
The morning mists would touch your sleeping heart
Before the dawn of light.
The days and nights of longing
Would vanish like the dew
There would be no waiting for tomorrow
If my heart could sing to you.

Butler family at Ione and Howard Hunt's wedding.

Bob Bradshaw on the bridge into Fairbank.

Bob on boat - 1924.

Alice Butler - 1924.

The Butler family
Back from left: Ione, Floyd, Jennie.
Front: Alice, Mr. and Mrs. Frank Butler and Minibel.

3

Our Wedding

June 5, 1926, our wedding day, finally arrived.

I awoke from a restless sleep, expecting a beautiful June day. To my horror, a strong wind drove pouring rain in sheets against our house.

I jumped out of bed and ran down the dark hall to Minibel's room. I slipped and fell, startling her awake. She opened her eyes to find me standing by the bed crying, my worries coming as fast as the rain outside. I felt certain Bob would never make it from Tilghman.

"For goodness sake," said Minibel, "sleet and snow never stopped him, so why worry about a little rain? Come on, sit down on the bed and dry your eyes."

She put her arms around me and gave me a big hug and smiled. "Hey, just think, if Bob doesn't come, we can still find our millionaire."

"That's not funny," I sniffed and wiped my eyes. "I want Bob, not a millionaire."

"It's going to be a beautiful day," she said jumping out of bed. "And Dad always says, rain is good for the crops. Come on, Sis, I'll beat you downstairs."

We found Mother in front of the fireplace. She had fashioned what resembled a small entrance to a path leading into the woods, gathered a wealth of arbutus which she intertwined with an arbor of ferns. The moist earth from the recent rain clung to the roots of the ferns. A woodsy fragrance filled the room. Mother always thought of details to complete a setting. She created a beautiful backdrop for our wedding.

I could see Mother had tears in her eyes and I knew she was thinking of her youngest leaving home. Our eyes met and suddenly we were in each other's arms. "Don't cry, mother, I'll be back home. It's only a hundred miles, you know."

Mother dashed her tears away and said, "I'm just being silly. Breakfast is ready. Come on, let's eat. We have a big day ahead of us.

A gust of wind accompanied Dad on his return from the morning's chores. "This rain is just what the crops need," he said and then must have seen my thoughts by looking at my face.

"Well Babe, are you ready for the big wedding today?" he said, giving me a hug. "Don't mind the rain, honey. Into everyone's life a little rain must fall," he quoted the old saying.

Mother put the sausage on the table while Minibel and I took turns baking pancakes. Dad said grace, and as we began to eat I realized that this was the last breakfast I would have with my family for a long time. Soon, I'd be in charge of breakfasts in my own kitchen.

Would I be as good a cook as Mother? What if I failed? And if we had children, would I be a good mother? Silently, I said a little prayer, "Dear God, help me to be a good wife and to be patient. Lord, you know I don't have much patience."

I felt better but I still had to excuse myself to keep from crying. As always, Minibel quickly saw how I was feeling. She jumped up and together we tackled the morning's dishes, letting the work keep our sad thoughts at bay.

The kitchen became a mass of confusion with everyone busy. Elmer arrived with fresh cream to go with strawberries from our garden into Mother's homemade ice cream. Dad worked with an ice pick on the block of ice in the ice box.

"Come on, Elmer," he said as the hired man turned to leave, "give this freezer a turn or you can't lick the beaters."

Minibel and I beat a hasty retreat out of the kitchen to clean the rest of the house. We weren't having a big wedding, just friends and neighbors from the community, but there were still many preparations. My brother, Floyd, and his family would be arriving later in the day.

Mother set the table with her beautiful linen cloth as she usually did for a special occasion. She had baked our wedding cake and decorated it with delicate orange blossoms and fragrant honeysuckle from her garden. The love that went into baking that cake meant more to me than a huge store-bought cake ever could have.

The ceremony was scheduled for two o'clock. At noon, there was still no sign of Bob, the preacher, or Bob's best man, Walter Lankford. What would I do if they didn't make it? I could picture myself sitting all alone in my wedding dress with all the food on the table, destined to be an old maid all my life.

Minibel rescued me from my dire thoughts. "Look, Sis, the rain is clearing up. Let's get upstairs before everyone gets here." She grabbed my arm and we flew upstairs just as Floyd's car drove up.

Our dresses lay on the bed. Minibel was my only attendant and her dress was a beautiful pale pink organdy which complimented her dark complexion.

My white silk dress was cut in princess lines. It was waltz-length with a ruffle around the bottom. I designed and made it myself with Mother's expert help. With justified pride, we thought it was lovely.

I had cut my hair in a short bob with ringlets around my face. I used a curling iron to make the curls. I heated its prongs in the chimney of the coal oil lamp. Clumsily, I tried to get the heat just right without burning my hair. Forgetting the iron for a moment, I turned to help Minibel fasten her dress. The smell of burning hair filled the air when I put it in the last curl. Quickly, I dropped the iron, but it was too late. The curl was gone. I started to cry.

"Oh, it looks horrible, doesn't it?" Minibel kidded. "Sit down and stop crying. I'll comb it so it will never show."

As always, Minibel came to my rescue. When Mother came in, the smell of burned hair was all that remained of the near-disaster. Mother looked elegant dressed in lavender and lace. At her throat, she wore a black velvet ribbon fastened with a silver double-heart clasp in the center.

She helped me into my dress and fastened a piece of lace taken from her trunk of treasures around my neck. Minibel loaned me her blue garter for good luck and I borrowed Jennie's veil. Preferring simple adornments, I wore only the pearl earrings and necklace Bob had given me,

We heard cars arriving in a steady stream for the ceremony. At last, among the voices below us, I picked out Bob's and Walter's voices. What a relief that I wouldn't be left at the altar! I thrust all thoughts of "old maids" from my mind. A knock on the door announced the arrival of our neighbor, Mrs. Bradly, with our flowers: Minibel's pink carnations and my white carnations, tied with a ribbon that trailed to the floor.

Mother looked at me, smiled and said, "You are a lovely bride, honey. Remember this day for the rest of your life and when things are rough, look back at your wedding vows. Keep them in your heart, walk with God and be happy."

My mother's words stayed with me all my life. They provided a bridge over troubled waters. In her wisdom, she knew the hardships of married life come to all of us. She and Dad experienced tough times, but through faith in God and themselves, they led happy lives and never faltered.

Mother put my bouquet of flowers in my arms and with a swift kiss, she left the room.

Minibel picked up her flowers, gave me a kiss and hug. "I love you, Sis," she said. Tears sprang to our eyes. I bowed my head into the sweet fragrance of my flowers, opened the door and stood at the top of the stairs.

Below, I could see the room filled with people and my legs started to shake. "I'll never make it to the bottom of these steps," I told myself as I pictured myself tumbling down the stairs in a pile of flowers and lost dignity.

Just then, the door to Mother and Dad's bedroom opened. Dad, in his black suit and tie, beamed proudly. As I took his arm, he leaned over, gave me a kiss, and whispered in my ear," You hold me up and I'll do the same for you, Babe."

We walked down the long stairs. God must have given me a push because I made it to Bob without a tremor. Waiting at the foot of the stairs, he looked so handsome in his blue serge suit with a carnation in his buttonhole.

Mother played the organ and sang "Oh Promise Me" as Bob took my hand. Through the warmth of his hand in mine, I felt the sacred trust we would share. In that moment, I knew that ours would be a marriage of eternity. I thought I was the luckiest girl in the world and I still do.

Halfway through the service, the sun broke through the clouds for a fleeting minute. A rainbow appeared in the clearing sky, then quickly vanished. The words, "Blessed is the bride the sun shines on" could not have carried more meaning than on this day I began my married life. Bob also must have been elsewhere with his thoughts, for he didn't say "I do". The minister continued the service without hesitation. Mother laughingly said afterwords to the minister, "Do you think they are truly married? Bob didn't say, "I do."

After two hours of festivities, we cut the cake and served refreshments. Minibel and I ran upstairs to change. She and Walter were accompanying us to the movies, a rare treat in those days and our only honeymoon! We couldn't spare money for any extravagance.

Ours was a working honeymoon and the only one we had until years later when our children were married. Patti, our second daughter, married Bill Tirschfield, a graduate from the Naval Academy in Annapolis, Maryland. While he was stationed in Germany, they invited us for a visit. It was a wonderful trip. We couldn't believe it was true. But the best of all was Mother's Day. When we came down for breakfast, a piece of paper lay on our plates. I supposed it was a card, but, no, when we opened it, it was a gift from Bill to visit Paris. On Patti's plate was a similar one to go with us. No words could describe our astonishment. All we could say was, "Thank you, thank you", over and over again with teary eyes and trembling voices. Our honeymoon had at last arrived. Although we didn't know it at the time, through the years, we would have many gifts from our children which took us all over the world. Could we ask God for anything more?

As luck would have it at that time, on the way to the movie theater in Cambridge, we got a flat tire. Bob and Walter fixed it in the pouring rain. Our "honeymoon" got off to a bumpy start!

Because of the raging storm, the streets were nearly deserted when we reached Cambridge. A few people splashed through the puddles with boots and umbrellas. When we reached the Arcade Theater, we parked the car and dashed in quickly. Just as we sat down, "The Trail of the Lonesome Pine" flashed across the screen. We feasted on popcorn and candy. Minibel and I were glad to see a movie about the mountains, since we remembered our western adventures in Montana. It told a wonderful love story about the family clans in Tennessee. A young engineer working in the mountains met a backwoods girl much younger than he. He taught her to read and write and encouraged her to go to school. Her friends and family didn't believe in education and laughed at her efforts. She persisted, even though they talked about her and shunned her ruthlessly. In later years, she taught school. She helped the children and older people live fulfilled, healthy lives. She eventually married the engineer and they became the light of the community.

The couple carved their names in a tall pine tree, a metaphor for their own lives: a lonesome pine standing alone reaching out its towering branches to the troubled. The couple believed in each other, even in troubling times. Life proved to be quite unlike this movie, but we were just starting a new course, so we held onto this standard. As the movie unfolded, Bob took my hand as he always did. I glanced across and saw that Minibel, usually so prim and proper, and Walter sat hand-in-hand also. I was happy that they had found love together, as we had.

When the movie ended, we emerged with high spirits, believing we could conquer anything. We stopped at the drugstore for sandwiches and ice cream. Bob had his favorite, a banana split, and I chose an ice cream soda. We joked and laughed until the manager looked our way, giving hints that it was time to close. Reluctantly, we buttoned our coats and stepped outside. Even though the rain continued, it didn't dampen our spirits. We were in love and felt all was right with the world. We arrived home late. Mother persuaded us not to drive to Fairbank until morning because of the bad weather. Bob hesitated, then agreed it would be best to wait.

After breakfast the next morning, Dad put our luggage in the car. We said our tearful goodbyes amid hugs and kisses. Minibel came over to the car and declared "I love you Sis." I turned my head so she couldn't see my tears. Bob started the car and we drove off to begin our life together on Tilghman Island at Fairbank. We had a long ride ahead of us. Mother packed us a lunch, and we stopped in a shady place and shared our first picnic as husband and wife. I felt excitement beyond words, like we were pioneers going west by wagon train as my mother did in the 1800's. A new life, I knew nothing about, with new challenges to face. I would get to test Mother's words when she said, "Learn to walk with God and be happy."

In the years to come, those words provided a firm foundation for a sound marriage. We depended on our wits and made our own decisions with God as our guide. We had no telephone to call home, but instead wrote letters through the long homesick days. Through trials, mistakes and many prayers, we learned the secrets of a happy marriage.

Federalsburg (Butler home)

Fireplace - drawn by Susanna Bradshaw Lang.

4

Our New Home

The storm that dampened our wedding day passed. The next day began with the sun ablaze in the sky, a new day and new life dawning for us. I am sure we were the happiest couple in the world. Of course, all married couples probably think this, but that day was particularly special to us after the years of separation and make-ups we had been through. I promised myself I wasn't going to be stupid and lose my temper anymore. I was a grown woman now. Tempers were for children. That was a hard promise to keep. I'm afraid Bob and I both broke our promise at times, but with God's grace, we had a life of excitement and love far beyond my fondest dreams.

In the late afternoon, we drove into the yard of our new home, bought for us by Bob's father, Captain Bain. My sister, Jennie, and her husband, Leslie, had lived there previously but no one had lived in it since then.

"Oh no", I cried in dismay when I saw the weeds that had grown up around it like a hay field. Bob quickly reassured me that he would have the weeds cut and grass mowed in no time.

"Didn't you know I'm a farmer as well as a waterman?" he said. "You just think about how beautiful it will be with flowers and shrubs and you and me in a hammock under the trees." He grinned and gave me a kiss. "But right now, let's jump out so I can take the car back to Dad's. We carried our luggage into the house. Bob set the suitcases on the floor, gave me a kiss, and promised to help cook supper when he came back from returning his father's car.

Jennie and Leslie had left some furniture so we would have something to start our home. She had left everything clean and neat. Of course, now dust was everywhere and the floors needed scrubbing, but that was nothing to me. After all, I grew up on a farm and was used to housework. The things I didn't know, I would learn.

The large kitchen was bright and sunny with yellow and green wallpaper to match the linoleum. Jennie had used it as a combination kitchen and dining room. Across the hall was the parlor. I walked up the stairs. The three bedrooms were tastefully papered with a bed and dresser in one room. I was relieved to know we wouldn't have to sleep on the floor. The windows in the bedroom were tall and reached the ceiling. None of the bedrooms had clothes closets but I couldn't be bothered about closets then.

I sat down for a few minutes, looking out at the weeds and high grass in the yard. Just as Bob had suggested, I began to dream. It was a nice big lot for a garden. I could imagine white curtains pulled back to let in the sun and air and through the window a freshly mowed lawn, an arbor over the kitchen door, and flowers all around the house.

Eventually, almost all my dreams came true. Bob built the arbor and I planted white clematis so that the fragrance drifted in through the kitchen door. I also planted flowers and shrubs along the garden fence. We made a simple home together.

I was still dreaming when Bob came in to tell me we had an invitation for supper at his father's house. We walked down the road, holding hands like two school kids. "I'm going to take off crabbing a few days to cut the grass and clean up the lot so we can plant a garden," he said. "It will be late, but who cares? I'll hire Mr. Frank Fairbank's mule and plow and I think I can get a scythe from Frank Fairbank to cut the weeds."

I didn't know any of the people he mentioned, so as we walked along, he slowed down and told me more about my new home and surroundings. He pointed out the people who lived on the road as we walked past: John and Ella Kapisak's home across the road from us, Captain Jim and Mrs. Dobson on our right, across the road, Captain Wood and Miss Florence Somers, next the Larrimore's and Nathan and Anna Parks. Bob's sister and brother-in-law, Minnie and Jim Price, lived in the last house. Finally we reached Tom Faulkner's store and post office where we had enjoyed ice cream on my earlier visits. Bob assured me I would soon know my neighbors.

We turned into his father's yard. We saw the boats anchored in the harbor. A light breeze rippled the surface of the water, sending little rivulets washing on the shore. All was peaceful and quiet. "Look at the sunset, honey", I said, and pointed to the horizon across the cove. Shades of yellow tinged the red sky and swept across the dark trees. We stood there a few minutes enthralled with the beauty of the evening.

"This is Black Walnut Cove," said Bob as we walked along the waterfront. He pointed out a large grey house on the other side where his Uncle Bill and Aunt Annie lived.

"That's enough for now. I'm hungry, let's go eat," Bob said and grabbed my arm. "Supper's ready."

I had only met Bob's mother and father once before this. His mother was paralyzed on one side of her body. Walking and talking were very difficult for her, but she managed with her family's help, especially Captain Bain's attentiveness to her. The four children at home also helped quite a bit. Mildred, a dark-haired teenager, always smiled. Myrtle, a fair child, was serious for her age, but always ready for a joke. Josephine's brown eyes sparkled. She stole your heart with her smile and laughter. To her friends and family, she was "Jo", but to her father, she was "Dinks". Bob's brother, Lloyd, was a young resemblance of Captain Bain: short, somewhat sturdy build with grey eyes glistening with mischief. He liked to play tricks on his sisters like all boys do. He reminded me of my brother, Floyd, a tease if there ever was one.

The girls kept the house sparkling clean and dressed their mother immaculately. Although Minnie had her own home next door, she was the key support of the family. She never failed to give a hand and words of encouragement to her mother and sisters; just being there was a blessing.

It was more difficult for Beatrice, another sister, to help, as she and her husband, Cooper Ball, lived about 12 miles away in

Neavitt, a small village near St. Michaels. They had three young daughters, Louise, Lazetta and Phyllis. Their grandmother enjoyed having them on weekends, and it gave the other girls time for themselves. In later years they all married except Phyllis. She entered Union Memorial Hospital to become a nurse. She served in the Korean War where she met and married Gene Evans.

There was always laughter and fun when the family gathered around the table, especially that night. I enjoyed being with the big family. It helped the homesick feeling in the pit of my stomach. I had been gone only a day, but I was already missing my family, especially Minibel and the long chats we used to have in our bedroom at night by the firelight. We kept the flames leaping high in the air until Dad came in and banked it down for morning.

Bob was up the next morning at dawn, not unusual for him. I lay there for a few moments, watching the sun peek through the windows, leaving the warmth on the bare floor. I threw my feet across the side of the bed, laughing at the clumsy sheet we strung over the bare glass to shield us from staring eyes the night before. Goodness, I would have to get busy making curtains!

"Honey, I have to run and pump out my boat. Then I'll attack those weeds in the garden while you cook breakfast," Bob said.

I finished dressing and went downstairs to start breakfast. I found a few essentials like canned milk, sugar and flour, together with the few groceries we bought with our last five dollars, I had enough to last until Friday, when Bob received his pay for crabs.

I wanted our first breakfast as a married couple in our own home to be absolutely perfect. I wore a beautiful pink plaid dress. I had bought it for my sparse trousseau, which to me seemed little more than a small wardrobe. I started breakfast on the coal oil stove. The tank was empty so I picked up a can from the two cans sitting together and filled the tank without looking at the label. I lit the wick and put the coffee on to boil, and I picked up a dishpan, filled it with water from the pump outside the door, and washed off the dusty table. I remembered the tablecloth I had tucked away in my beautiful solid oak hope chest Dad made for each of we girls as wedding gifts. I set the table with all the care of a banquet. Since I had no flowers for our centerpiece, I found a pretty bowl in the cupboard and filled it with oranges. We had everyday pieces of china from broken sets we had collected.

Bob would always exclaim, "Oh honey, we don't have much money, but you set the table like a king was coming to supper!"

And I would always blush, "A king is coming: you."

I guess my mother had taught me well, for he seemed impressed by my efforts. My mother treated my father the same way and always insisted that everything be in its proper place. My father served the food on Sundays, whether we had company or not.

My first morning's breakfast proved to be a complete disaster however. I was so preoccupied with setting the table artfully, that I never thought of the stove until I heard the coffee boil over. Smoke billowed out of the chimney and filled the room with soot. I panicked and ran to the stove and tried to turn the burners off, but they burned my hands. I knocked the coffeepot over and spilled hot black coffee all over my nicely scrubbed floor. The room filled with smoke and soot and I could hardly breathe. I ran out into the yard and screamed for Bob. He thought the house was on fire and came running. He slipped on the coffee splattered on the floor and muttered something unprintable. He saw where the fire came from and muffled it with a towel, then he glared at me.

"What in the world happened?" he asked bluntly.

"I don't know. I filled the tank and lit the stove like I was supposed to do," I replied, full of confusion.

Then he saw the oil can. "Did you fill the tank with that oil?" he demanded.

"Yes, the tank was empty", I answered.

"Honey, that is gasoline and this is a coal oil stove!" He looked at me and burst out laughing.

"What's so funny? I nearly burned the house down!" I said indignantly.

"Look at yourself in the mirror!" he said. I looked and my face, arms, and my beautiful pink dress were covered with soot. I was black enough for a masquerade comedy skit and nearly crying with the tragedy of it all.

"I wanted everything to be so perfect! How could I be so stupid?" I wondered aloud. Bob cleaned the stove, put the proper oil in the tank and heated water to wash off. With lather all over my face and arms, I was soon presentable. We spent the rest of the day scrubbing the walls, furniture and floor, not quite what I had envisioned for our first day! Bob never tired of telling the story and how funny I looked covered with black soot.

The rest of the week passed uneventfully. Bob returned to crabbing. When he went out the door, he kissed me and made me promise not to burn the house down while he was gone. I threw a towel at him, promising to learn about the stove, even if it took a lifetime.

The weekly routines took shape quickly. On Mondays, I washed clothes. Bob filled two large lard cans with water to heat on the stove. I boiled the clothes in the cans then scrubbed them on the washboard. I repeated this in another tub of rinse water, then blued them to keep them white. This proved quite a task for a new bride! I learned slowly but surely. Everyone did their clothes the same way, so I accepted it.

I failed completely the first time I tried to hang the clothes on the line! The wind blew wildly: I didn't know where to begin. I fumbled and threw the sheets over the line, but the wind was too quick. My neighbor, Addie Cummings, who was Bob's cousin, saw me wrestling with the sheets and came to rescue me. She deftly caught the corners together by the hems and neatly hung them on the line. "You see if you don't hang them by their hems the wind will whip the hems out," she said. So much for my first lesson.

I had many more lessons to learn in the years to come. I thanked her and from that day on, I thanked God for good neighbors. Through the years, we became fast friends and our children played and fought together like siblings.

By the end of the month, I knew most of the people in our small community. In the beginning, we had no electricity or plumbing. The pump was outside the door and our bathroom, or privy, was at the end of the lot. We had to travel so far from the house that winter blasts froze us and the sizzling heat and mosquitoes of summer drove us to exasperation. Some good arose out of this situation, however, as I usually could stop and talk to a neighbor passing by. I also learned that gossip travels fast in a small town!

Eventually, Bob piped the water into the house and the pump became our faucets. What a joy to have a sink and a pump. I didn't have to stand in the freezing rain to thaw out the pump any more. The children used the sink as a bathtub while they were small but the washtub was ours. In the winter, we set it in the middle of the floor beside the roaring fire, but we had to lock the doors or we'd be invaded with pattering feet.

I helped Bob plant the garden and mow the lawn. Only one eyesore remained. At the end of our lot, a Ford parts sign spoiled the beauty. I asked Adam Kapisak who owned the sign if I could plant a bush there and he consented. We had a spot of color and a rest for my eyes after I planted a forsythia. This road led to Kapisak's Marine Railway, the only blacksmith on that end of the Island. The Kapisaks who kept a store were on the same road as Captain Earn Jenkins and Miss Rose who became some of my dearest friends. Miss Rose had a speech defect and a hearing handicap which made it very difficult for me to understand her. She read lips though, so soon we learned to understand each other. No one had a dearer or truer friend.

Eventually, we put our "starter" furniture aside and bought some of our own.

First we bought a secondhand wicker set with red plush cushions for twenty-five dollars for the parlor. I coaxed Bob into helping me measure the windows. My white dotted swiss curtains with valances and ties to let in the breeze became a reality. Bob's parents presented us with a solid oak bedroom set. The varnished oak floors, adorned with the braided rugs from home, made a beautiful room of which we were very proud. My mother and Dad gave us a Queen Anne dining room suite which we put at one end of the parlor for Sundays. We bought an unpainted kitchen set and I painted it a cream color and put decals on the table and backs of the chairs. We added a kitchen cabinet, a revelation to me: a place for dishes, a work table, and a small cabinet for flour with a flour sifter!

By winter, we needed a wood cookstove. We looked through our old trusty Sears catalog and found a cookstove the same color as our light cream cabinet. I wanted to cook all the time! We also had a warming oven and hot water tank. As all watermen, Bob never adhered to a schedule for coming home. They worked on a schedule which varied according to the weather. By dawn, they were out in their boats, unless a gale of wind held them back. Meals could wait for hours, so a warming oven was convenient.

We always carried our coal stove out in the garage for the summer and used an oil stove to cook on. Our kitchen became a living room or dining room when we had company for the summer. Beside the back door was a breezeway connected to an outside kitchen which we used in the summer to cook and the breezeway was a dining room. It was screened in and a lovely place to eat.

Captain and Mrs. Bain Bradshaw.
(Courtesy of Carroll Wesley Newcomb.)

**Our new home at Fairbank.
(Drawing by Susanna Bradshaw Lang.)**

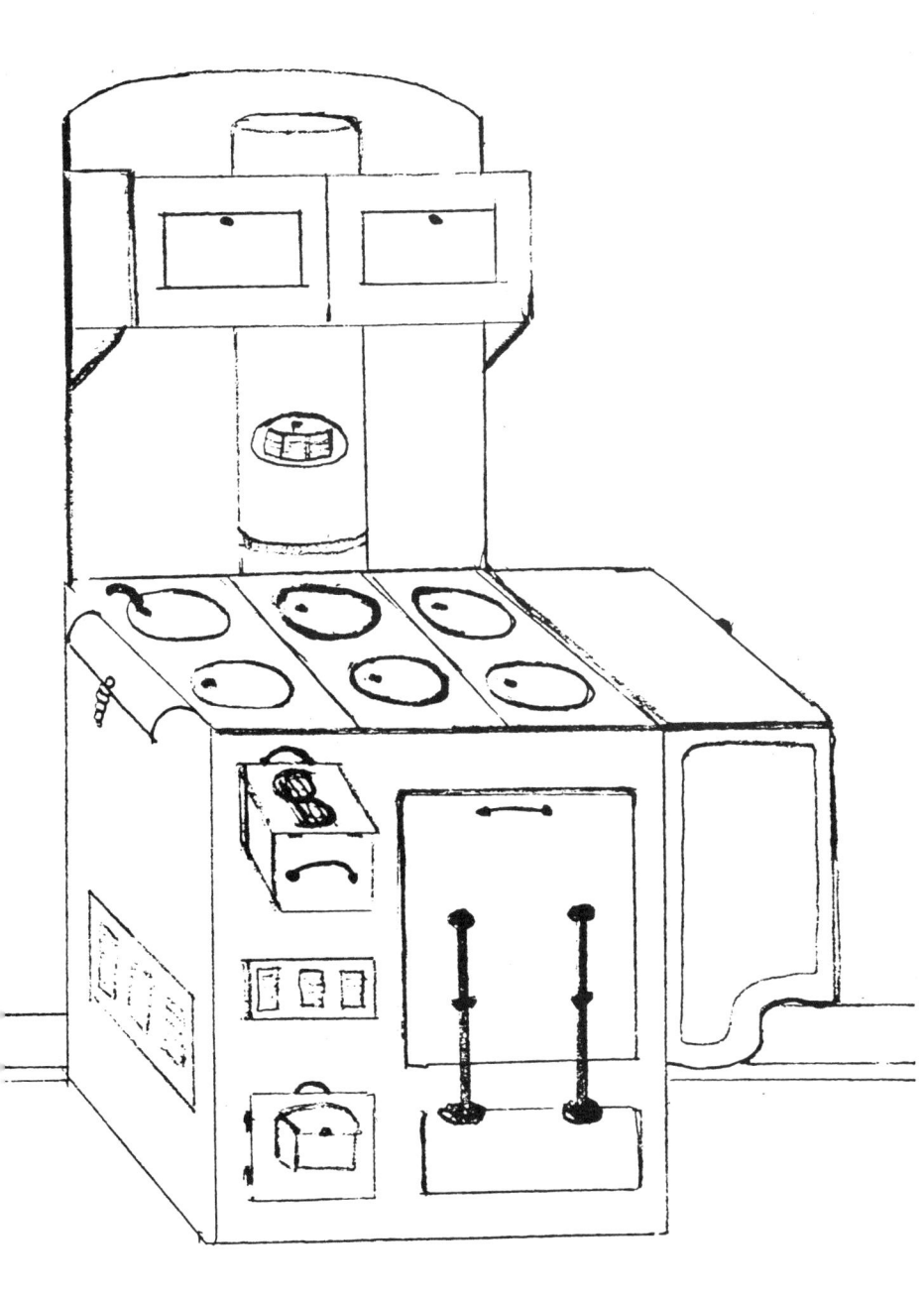

**Our first cookstove.
(Drawing by Susanna Lang.)**

5
The Village of Fairbank

In the weeks that followed, I learned the ways of life and the people of this fishing village. These hard-working families earned their daily living from the Chesapeake: oystering, fishing and crabbing.

The men congregated in Tom Faulkner's store after supper each evening. They gathered to swap tales, true and false, who knows? They settled scores by a bet: who would catch the most oysters, who had the fastest sailing boat, or who would win the Presidential election. Many fights broke out between Democrat and Republican.

A big pot-bellied stove stood in the center of Faulkner's store surrounded by a bed of sawdust. This caught trash of any kind, as well as tobacco juice, which hit the stove with a sizzle and a smell that permeated the room. Raucous curses and swearing scorched the air, but when a woman's footsteps were heard outside, all was quiet until she left. Then again, their rowdy voices rang out. The men respected women at all times; I never heard a swear word in front of a lady.

As a boy, Bob sneaked out of the house to sit and listen to their tales. When he was missed at home, Captain Bain grabbed him by his shoulders and marched him home. Bob would climb a pole in the middle of the room after the men greased it and placed a coin on top. If he reached the top, they threw him pennies for spending money. Also on Halloween night, if he was missed at home, his sisters dressed a scarecrow and stood it at the door. Another time, when he went to bed, they had put a dummy in his bed. That kept him at home for a long time. He was afraid to venture out at night. The store didn't tempt him for a long time. Minnie was a big tease, always playing jokes.

Captain Larry and Miss Laura Faulkner ran the only boarding house in Fairbank at that time. I don't know how many years it had been operating before I lived there. People from Baltimore, Washington, D.C., and Pennsylvania came during the summers, year after year, for rest and recreation. Some stayed the whole summer, others for a week or two. At night, we heard singing and dancing from the Faulkners' guests. Miss Laura had a player piano which entertained the guests late into the night. Captain Earn Jenkins took fishing parties from the boarding house.

Bob described the hay rides that he went on, accompanied by some of the girls he knew before we were married. Judging by his stories, they had rough rides and exciting times. I teased him about his old girlfriends, but he laughed it off. "I might have gone with a lot of girls, honey, but I married you didn't I?" he declared.

"I know," I said, "but see what a dull life you have now."

He grabbed me and said, "Honey, I knew I was going to marry you that first night we met. Don't you ever forget that. Forget those girls and let's go to bed."

Captain Laury kept the largest garden in the community. He planted or hoed in the early morning hours, then took a break until late afternoon and worked again until dark. I don't think Miss Laura ever went anywhere. She contented herself with her life and work in their lovely home on the water.

One of Bob's good friends was Hedge, one of four grown children of Mr. Frank and Miss Annie Fairbank, who had a farm but lived in Fairbank. Two of the other children, Bill and Hazel, lived in Baltimore, and the fourth child, Roland. worked on the water. Bob and Hedge freighted, or "ran" oysters together.

Miss Rose taught me Island cooking. I thought I could cook anything, but I didn't know the particular nuances of Island cooking. For example, Bob didn't like vegetables cooked in a cream sauce which was the only way I knew how to fix vegetables. I consulted Miss Rose who shared the Island secret that a piece of bacon or ham spiced up the vegetables.

Bit by bit, I learned the culinary art of shortbread and sweet potato pie. I learned how to pick crabs and make crab cakes. Cakes and pies gave me no trouble, although my first cake could have substituted for a baseball! After that humbling experience, I wrote to Mother for cake recipes. I still bake using many of her recipes. Bob teasingly said, "Honey, your apple pie is almost as good as your mother's."

I soon learned the ways of life in a small community. I learned to walk the straight and narrow path and weigh my words carefully before I said them. By the time something was repeated around the community, it was usually blown completely out of proportion, until the person wondered how they ever said such a thing! The gossipers knew your personal business before you did. Other people came readily in times of need. The good outweighed the bad and we thanked God for both. Now, looking back, I think it was the best part of my life. I have lived on two islands during my life. Each of them taught me that the highs and lows depend on your actions.

On the corner past the church sat an old abandoned building. High weeds covered the yard. Bob said that it had been Mr. Walter Weber's store years ago. When his children married and moved away, the store closed. The upstairs was used for community parties and church suppers. The stairs were on the outside of the building. An old pump was still in use beside the door, overgrown with weeds. It saddened me to see something so useful gone to ruin.

One day, as we walked home from church, Bob said, "Hey, honey, maybe in a few years we could buy it and have an ice cream parlor there?"

"Yeah," I said, "and the kids would eat up all the profit."

"Don't be silly," he laughed, "we're going to have nice kids who wouldn't do such a thing. That's a long way down the road anyway, but we can dream, can't we?"

"Sure, honey," I said. "You know me; I'm a dreamer. Mother always told me to work for a good cause. If it doesn't work out, she reminded me that there is a silver lining." Mother's silver lining was God. She depended and trusted in Him. At the end of every letter she wrote, she included a thought for the day, usually a scripture to carry me over the rough places in life.

One evening we walked around to Black Walnut Point on the Bay. We waded along the beautiful sandy beach. Bob said, "You know, out there was a big field of tomatoes I helped plant. Where the water is now, this used to be fields of wheat, too."

He wanted me to meet his Aunt Annie down the road. The Bay glistened in the sunlight, whitecaps rising and falling as the wind blew in a rhythm all its own. He pointed to the lighthouse which was in full view from where we stood.

"That was land too at one time," he narrated.

"I wish there had been land when you took _me_ up there!" I exclaimed.

"It's much more fun this way, don't you think?" he said. "Do you want to go again?"

"No, thank you," I replied hastily. "I've had enough lighthouses for a lifetime."

Finally, we reached Aunt Annie's yard. She sat under the tree picking crabs and invited us to sit down. Although she was elderly, her eyes sparkled and lit up her whole face when she smiled. Aunt Grace came out to invite us for dinner. No one ever left their house without eating, even if you were already full. So we stayed for supper. Grace turned out to be one of the happiest people I met, with honesty and merriment written all over her face.

We walked home in the dusk, the fireflies lighting our way, as they did the night we met. Bob showed me where the Fluhartys lived. He showed me where Miss Rose Tyler, who had been the midwife of Fairbank, lived. All babies were born at home at that time. She brought many babies into the world with a doctor's help.

Later, when Dr. Guy Reiser came to the Island from the hills of Tennessee, his wife worked as his helper. He was the most dedicated doctor I have ever known; timing was never too early or too late for him. He came within minutes, unless he was with another patient. Often, people didn't have money to pay him, but he never sent a bill. His office calls cost five dollars and delivering a baby cost twenty-five dollars. Once a year, he went to homes to collect. He seemed to have vast knowledge in the medical field. He knew by the shade of your skin if you had cancer before it was ever diagnosed. Although he swore and had a "rough" manner, it never interfered with his abilities to treat people. We felt fortunate to have a doctor in any case.

I remember one time Bob's brother, Lloyd, and Bernard Koffman were playing ball. They ran into each other and Bernard's teeth sunk into Lloyd's forehead. Blood gushed all over and Bob fainted, as he always did when he saw blood. Dr. Reiser came and found Bob and Lloyd out cold on the ground. He took one look and swore, "Who the hell is sick here?"

After throwing a pitcher of ice water in Bob's face to revive him, he found out that Lloyd was hurt. Dr. Reiser took Lloyd into the house and sewed up the cut, leaving a permanent scar.

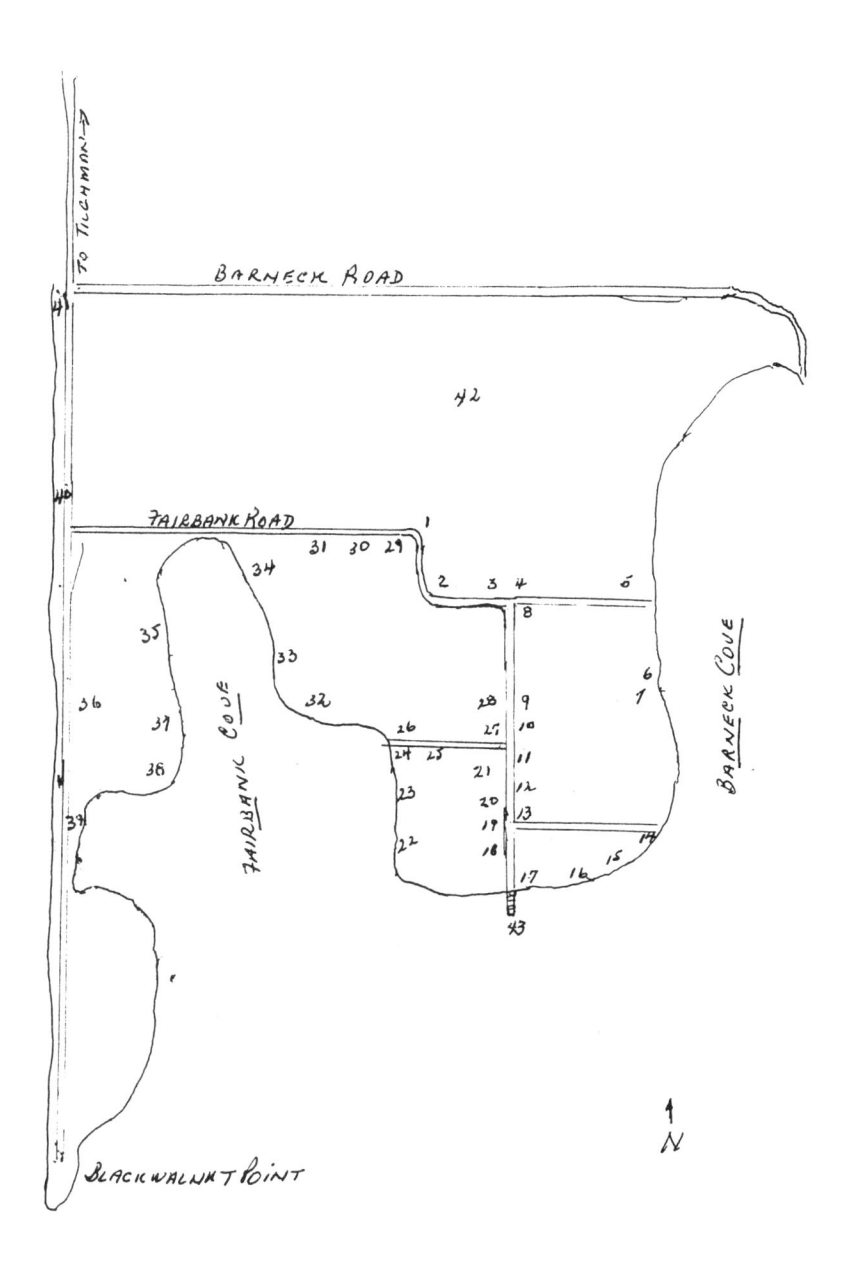

Map of Fairbank.
(Supplied by Gorman Cummings.)

Fairbank Village - 1930

1. Schilling Bozman
2. Chapel Church
3. Frank Howeth
4. Paul Kapisak
5. Faulkner Boarding House
6. Roland Fairbank
7. Frank Fairbank
8. Weber's Store and Hall
9. John Kapisak
10. Wood Somers
11. Glendy Larrimore
12. Nathan Parks
13. James Price
14. Fairbank Crab House
15. Caroll McQuay
16. Roland McQuay
17. Jacob Bain Bradshaw
18. Faulkner Store
19. Tom Faulkner
20. George Roe
21. Jim Dobson
22. Ed McQuay
23. Bob Kapisak
24. Railway - Adam Kapisak
25. Kapisak Store
26. Earn Jenkins
27. Bob Bradshaw
28. Gorman Cummings
29. Elish Cummings
30. Clem
31. Clarence Harrison
32. George Cummings
33. Adam Kapisak
34. Walter Weber
35. John Grunski
36. Lewis Fluhart
37. Rose Tyler
38. Tom Parks
39. William Henry Bradshaw
40. Ed Harrison
41. St. Johns Church
42. Sinclair Farm
43. County Dock

Names supplied by Gorman Cummings.

**Addie and Gorman Cummings home.
(Courtesy of Gorman Cummings.)**

Main Street, Fairbank, Maryland.

Tom Faulkner's Store and Post Office. (Courtesy of Bernard Kauffman.)

Frank Fairbank's house.

Privy
(Photo courtesy of Gorman Cummings.)

County whart at Fairbank looking north around 1930.
(Courtesy Bernard Kauffman.)

6

The Little Chapel and Ladies Aid

Some people attended the Little Chapel at the bend of the road, but most of the people from Barneck attended St. John's Church across the road from Barneck Road. Bob's family attended St. John's. His cousin, Addie Cummings, and his Uncle Bill Bradshaw's family did also. Bob and I attended the Little Chapel because most of our neighbors went there.

I only knew the people from Barneck through the Ladies Aid even though it was just another part of Fairbank, separated by a small cove of water. It was too far to walk. We had no transportation, except for an occasional visit by boat. Nonetheless, the communities felt closely knit. The churches worked together with the Ladies Aid.

Each family contributed to the church regardless of whether they attended services. They made a commitment to share with God and with each other. Those who didn't attend regularly gave money and helped repair and maintain the church. Once a month, several members collected money through the community for the minister's salary. We always met our commitment, although there were hard times when it was hard to give.

Everyone walked to church. We had two ministers, one for each church. A month after our wedding, we started going to church. Myrtle Kapisak, one of the hardest workers in the church, came by and invited us. I had attended church all my life and I missed it sorely. Church was a part of my life that I could never have functioned without. From the day we joined, we never missed a church service except for sickness or inclement weather. Because the minister had two other charges to hold services, our service was at two o'clock in the afternoon.

The first Sunday at church, the ringing bell seemed to whisper, "Now you are back. Live here and be happy. When life grows weary, remember the Lord." There were times in the following years we felt the whole world toppled on our shoulders, but the ringing bell beckoned us to the quiet little church on Sundays.

Although only twelve or fifteen people attended each Sunday, we shared a comraderie of happiness and mutual concern. Our church was a simple place, but to Bob and me, it was a restful place by the side of the road where we could leave our burdens of the week. The church rang with singing voices in praise of God. Our problems seemed to fade away. We could face another week, spiritually refreshed and ready for challenges.

Traditions on the Island included Children's Day and Mother's Day. The three churches, Tilghman, St. John's, and the Little Chapel, celebrated on different Sundays, so the people could attend each one. We usually attended St. John's and the Little Chapel's programs.

We planned the program at the Ladies Aid meetings, deciding who would be chairman and who would volunteer to train the children. I enjoyed helping. It was quite a task, but a work of love. If you ever attended one you would say so too.

It took two or three weeks to prepare the church and the children. We all lost our patience at times and would have gladly thrown it all down, but no way could Children's Day be avoided.

We decorated the church the same as for Christmas, but with wild flowers and morning glory vines across the platform forming a welcome banner. Flowers in baskets adorned the platform and altar. Their perfume filled the air with the rich fragrance of roses and honeysuckle.

The program came together beautifully. I can still see the church and the children dressed so fancily climbing the steps to the platform. We wouldn't have thought of putting our girls in anything but frilly dresses, hats, gloves, and either black patent leather or white slippers. The boys looked handsome in their pressed blue serge suits and ties.

Sometimes the toddlers forgot their speeches and ran down to the comfort of their mother's arms. The shining faces left a tear in your eye and a warm spot in your heart.

On Mother's Day the older people took part in a similar program along with the children. I loved seeing the church so crowded because usually only about fifteen people attended on Sundays.

Once a year, during the early fall days each church had revival services. They were always packed to capacity. Ministers who had preached there before were invited to preach. I learned the old hymns of the church. I remember standing in the church filled with people singing the old hymns which have been passed down through the ages. It inspired and uplifted our hearts and souls for weeks to come.

The Little Chapel badly needed a new roof and interior paint when Reverend Charles W. Atkins came to be the minister in 1927. He proved to be an ambitious and skilled carpenter, as well as a minister. He did much of the remodeling work to supplement his salary.

He replaced the roof and repaired the windows to keep them from leaking. He made high screens for the windows so that we could raise them to let in cool air on hot days. Even when the temperature soared upwards of 100 degrees, the cross breeze and the slow-moving woven fans kept us cool.

Reverend Atkins arranged for a new floor of solid oak to be laid. We varnished and polished it until it shone like a fountain of water. We laid a deep red carpet from the door to the Communion railing encasing the whole platform. Red velvet-covered pulpit chairs lent a soft elegance. A beautiful chandelier, with lights shaped like gleaming candles, hung in the center. Along the walls, the same "candles" glowed at evening service. Small tinted lights, styled in a cross, set forth a beacon of light as you entered the door. Fresh oyster white paint graced the walls and old-fashioned metal ceiling carved in an intricate pattern.

To me, the Chapel was a castle where I could go on Sundays or any day of the week to talk to God and renew life. Today, years later, I remember its beauty and simplicity vividly.

Even today, years after we left the Island, our church life is ingrained in my memory. Its beauty and quietness go with me. I wish our children could have grown up there, to know and love the simple ways of life. We freely brought our babies and felt no intrusion from the congregation. Those who didn't attend services sent their children faithfully to church and Sunday school. Their respect and love of God was their background.

Mr. Walter Weber and his wife Minnie donated the land for the church. They were faithful keepers of the church both in attendance and money. He was Sunday School Superintendent for many years. After he died, Mr. Jim Callis took over. Bob was elected when Mr. Callis died.

Social activity on the Island revolved around the Ladies Aid. Each church, St. John's and the Little Chapel, both worked for each of their own church but the Ladies Aid was combined. Without the support of the Ladies Aid and their work towards the upkeep of the church building, the church couldn't exist. The Tilghman Church had a separate Ladies Aid, but they worked with both churches, such as always respecting special days so that dates didn't conflict. All three churches worked together cleaning the Parsonage when a new minister came.

We worked together on quilts to raffle off at our oyster suppers. Also, we raised money for church expenses and for needy families in the community.

I joined the Ladies Aid soon after we were married and became friends with all the members. Since most of the ladies in the community belonged to the group, I could meet many of the families in Bar Neck. Each family took turns having the monthly meetings at their home. We always eagerly anticipated that one night of the month.

The social hour followed the business meeting. Fun was the name of the game. We had singalongs and comedy skits that left us in laughter and tears.

We played games like "My Aunt Sarah Died." We needed to have all of our wits together to play this game because by the time it was half over, our sides hurt from laughing. All the participants sat in a circle. The leader said to the person on her right, "My Aunt Sarah died."

Ladies repeated this phrase all around the circle. When it reached the leader, the next person said to the leader, "What did she die of?"

The leader said, "With her mouth awry and her hand on high." This circulated through the ladies, each one holding a position with her mouth awry and hand on high, if they could.

The next question to the leader was, "How did my Aunt Sarah die?"

The person responded, "With her mouth awry, her hand on high, and foot pointing to the sky." Each asked the same question and kept their position, adding the new element. By this time, everyone was laughing and trying to hold their position. The one who held their position the longest won a funny prize. Whenever we needed a good laugh, this game would be hilarious.

For refreshments at the meetings, people served lemonade, iced tea and coffee, as this was before the soft drink rage. We served homemade ice cream and cake to top off the evening of work and fun.

When my turn came for the monthly meeting, I thought I had everything in order. Since I was entertaining for my first time, I wanted everything to go perfectly.

We made the ice cream ahead of time. Bob turned the freezer while I cleaned and baked cakes. Bob put the freezer outside on the steps to keep the water from the melted ice from running onto the freshly scrubbed floor. When it was time for refreshments, I opened the door to find the ice cream gone. I looked all over the ground. No ice cream. I didn't say anything; I was so embarrassed. What would everyone think of a hostess who served cake and no ice cream?

After a few moments, there was a miraculous knock on the door and when I opened it, I heard running feet. On the step was my freezer, just like it had been, not even opened. I turned around and with a grateful laugh, I said, "Well ladies, time for ice cream."

Someone helped me lift the freezer. As I related what had happened, everyone laughed heartily, but it wasn't funny to me. I never knew who the culprits were, but I'm sure it was a bunch of kids playing a joke. Everyone went home happy. Even I could laugh by that time. As usual, there would be flaws in my best plans, but in the end, it came out all right.

Ladies Aid always held a summer picnic. One of the oyster houses loaned us a truck and driver so we could go to a nearby farm. We all packed our own lunches, but set everything out on the ground so we could enjoy each other's goodies. If we were lucky, we had the use of a long table. We feasted on fried chicken, ham sandwiches, pickles, tomatoes, potato salad, and homemade ice cream and cake for dessert.

(This book's third printing contains a new poem on page 209, *Memories of St. John's Chapel,* **by Alice B. Bradshaw.)**

Little Chapel - 1884.
(Courtesy of Lula Mae Weller.)

St. John's Methodist Church
(Courtesy of Lula Mae Weller.)

7

Crabbing Season and Summer Reverie

The crabbing season began in June. The first morning, it seemed like the middle of the night when I heard the alarm go off; it wasn't even daylight! Bob jumped out of bed, grabbed his clothes and lit the lamp. I glared at the clock which read "4:00 a.m."

"You didn't warn me you were leaving so early," I said.

"I have to," he declared, pulling a T-shirt over his head. "The crabs are better on the Western Shore, so I'm going to beat everyone there and be home by early afternoon."

I reminded him of his lunch which I had packed the night before. I had given him enough for breakfast and lunch. When I asked him how many sandwiches he wanted, he had said "Oh, a loaf, I guess."

"A whole loaf of bread?"

"Sure," he said, "I won't eat any more until supper. That's not much for a big fellow like me."

Bob *was* big. He measured six feet tall with broad shoulders and hands that doubled the size of mine. Watermen needed hands and muscles of steel for their strenuous work. Although they acted tough one minute, they could be as docile as a lamb the next.

I turned over as Bob left the room, hoping to get a couple more hours of sleep. I dozed off to the tramp, tramp of feet on the oyster shell road and the chug, chug of motors as each crabber went where they thought the crabs would be biting.

Crabbing was done with a trot line, a long, one-half inch rope, one hundred to three hundred feet long. The crabbers placed snoozers which are short pieces of crabbing cord, about twelve inches long. They are pushed through the crab line, tied securely with a slipknot at its end. The salt eel bait was placed inside the slipknot then pulled tightly. They coiled the rope in the crab barrels so they could run it through a chalk line on the side of the boat. They fastened a float to each end of the line then threw it overboard.

The men ran their boats out to the end of the line. Then as they came back, they used a dip net to dip the crabs as they grabbed for the bait. For soft-shelled crabs, they pushed their row boat along the shore and dipped the net into the sea grass where the soft crabs hid until their shells grew hard enough to swim.

Fathers passed on the art of crabbing, like dredging or fishing, to their sons at an early age. Since I had never seen them working before, I found watching crabbers fascinating.

Crabs brought decent money for the times; a dollar to a dollar and a half a barrel. Lucky crabbers got ten or twelve barrels a day. Soft crabs brought a better price. It wasn't much for a twelve-hour day. By the time you bought bait and gasoline, there wasn't much profit. In rainy or windy weather, crabs didn't bite, so the men stayed home.

Crabbing provided us with a good living our first summer. Bob built a float for his soft crabs and made good money. We were able to make the first payment on our home. We started saving a little money so Bob could buy a boat of his own. Our large garden furnished us with all we could eat and can for winter. We felt on top of the world! Life was at a peak of goodness and we were grateful.

After crabbing season, Bob wanted me to go with him to freight wheat to Baltimore. Another big step for me, from oysters to wheat! I was unsure about going, but in the end Bob got his way and I started another chapter in the story of my sea life.

Captain Jim Dobson owned a large sailing boat but was getting too old to freight wheat by himself. He needed a younger man like Bob to help with the lifting.

I found this to be much more exciting than freighting oysters. We sailed down the Bay to the farmlands on the water. There the wheat was loaded onto the boat. Captain Jim laid back and slept while Bob handled the steering. He taught me how to steer by using a certain point ahead and how to dodge other boats coming or going.

One time, a thunderstorm came up and Bob had to reef the sails to keep from going over. Although I felt really scared, I was thankful to have such a skilled sailor in charge. The boat rode the crashing waves, but they rose so high that they washed over the boat. The wind lashed viciously against the sails until Bob got them all down and secured. Captain Jim came out of the cabin to help. Bob sent me down to the cabin so I wouldn't be washed overboard. Thunder and lightning crashed all around us. Bob gripped the wheel to keep the boat on course. Each time we went down, I thought it was the end and we would sink to the bottom of the Bay. Captain Dobson slipped and almost fell overboard. Bob grabbed him and sent him down to the cabin with me.

"I'll take care of the boat," he told Captain Jim. I'm sure he prayed fervently and I know I did.

I remember this as the worst storm I ever endured. At the time, I hoped it would be the last! Gradually, the storm passed and all was quiet again. We crawled cautiously out of the cabin because the waves persisted, high and choppy.

"You're quite a skipper, my boy," said Captain Dobson putting his hands on Bob's shoulders. "I'm glad I brought you along."

Bob grinned and shrugged off the praise. "It wasn't so bad," he said. "I've seen worse."

Sailing up the Bay was much different from sailing to Cambridge. We passed steamships from foreign ports being towed into the harbor. They looked so big beside our boat. I felt as though we would be sucked under by the huge waves that came from their motors. Sounds of chugging tugboat engines and their horns blowing as they made their way into Baltimore filled the air. The steamships looked like floating cities when you saw them lit up at night.

As we sailed into Baltimore, we threw the anchor lines onto the wharf at the grain elevators. The big pipes vacuumed the wheat like magic into the storage bins ashore. At night, we walked uptown to buy goodies to take with us on the boat. What a treat to see all of the sights of the city! We didn't buy much, but enjoyed window shopping and dreaming.

We usually sailed back to the Island the next day. We settled in to wait for another call from the farmers. I always appreciated setting my feet on solid ground. I didn't think I'd ever get totally accustomed to life as a sailor.

"I'm still staggering and feel like I will fall on my head any moment," I told Bob. "My head is full of motor sounds and I'm weird all over."

"Don't worry," said Bob, pulling me down on his lap. "By the end of the season, you'll be an accomplished seawoman. You aren't always going to be a creampuff. One of these days, you'll pull a sail down like I do."

"I don't know," I said. "Right now, all I want to do is crumple up and go to sleep."

He sent me upstairs to take a nap. "I'll cook supper," he said. "I can cook as well as you can!"

And he could too!

A crabber at work with a dip net and crab barrel.

8
The Oyster Season

The oyster season started in November. Weeks before dredging, the captains lined up their dredge boats in the harbor. In the early morning, I heard the sound of feet on the road. Sometimes, they stumbled as their feet hit a pile of oyster shells.

The men dressed in oilskin coats, felt boots and rubber gloves to protect their hands from the rough oyster shells and the harsh cold. The crews and captains untied the rowboats at the dock and slowly rowed out to their boats in the harbor. There, the cook already had a hearty breakfast prepared for the hungry men.

They kept a supply of food on board. Each week, the men bought supplies at Tom Faulkner's general store, like flour, sugar, dried beans, fatback, bacon sides, dried fruit, rice, large beef roasts and canned milk. They prepared surprisingly good food in the tiny pilot house: shortbread baked in the top of a lard can, corned beef hash and bean soup.

Water flowed from Captain Bain's spring to a connecting pipe that extended to the water's edge. This supplied water to the dredge boats. As a small boy, Bob filled jugs with fresh water then rowed them out to the boats and filled the water barrels. He also sold "Grit" magazine and the Sunday newspaper because they had no radios or newscasts. He enjoyed these simple tasks that helped the men with their work.

I soon learned all there was to know about dredging! On each side of the boat, a dredge attached to a winder which they operated by hand. The men threw these dredges overboard. As the boat sailed over the oyster beds, the dredges scraped oysters from the bottom of the Bay. The men hauled in the dredges and dumped the oysters on board so they could cull them. They shoveled the small ones back into the water. Then the legal size oysters were piled in four piles to keep the boat balanced. They sold the oysters to a packing house or sold them to buy boats in the harbor.

Bob freighted oysters when we were married. He was tired of the relentless back-breaking work on the deck of a boat. On the first day of dredging, he asked me to go along with him on the boat.

"Me on a boat? No thank you," I said. "I'll stay home and keep house."

"Come on," he pleaded. "It'll be fun, just you and me out on the Chesapeake."

"Out on the Chesapeake, that's what frightens me," I said, remembering our harrowing adventure at the lighthouse. "I don't like the thought of all that water around me. Besides, whoever heard of a woman working on a buy boat?"

"*You* can be the first," he said.

I accepted the challenge. Bundled up to my ears in a warm coat and scarf, I stumbled along beside him until we reached the water's edge. I had no idea of the cold and blustery wind until I stepped aboard the boat. Though the water still frightened me, I sailed with him on the boat, "The Josephine". I soon found that the Chesapeake wasn't my only problem; I was the talk of the town. Some people approved of me working with Bob on the boat and some didn't. I felt that as long as Bob wanted me to go, that was their problem.

Many times I regretted ever setting foot on a boat. The first time proved to be awful. The salty, dead air of the cabin nearly turned my stomach, but I was determined to be a sailor. After Bob built a fire in the cook stove, everything became cozy and warm. I relished the days when the Bay was calm and we used the motor instead of the sail.

Most of all, I dreaded the storms on the Chesapeake with the ferocious winds, rain, snow and blizzards to sail through. We blazed through them together and I'm glad I had the courage to go along. I forgot the hardships and we enjoyed being together. Now I realize that I forged a radical path by accompanying him to work.

I'll never forget the first time the wind really blew a fierce gale. We were freighting oysters between Tilghman and Cambridge, which was about an hour and a half sail. When the wind came up, Bob ordered me to retreat to the cabin below. He felt no fear. He had been raised on the water and went ahead with his work in spite of storms or hazards of any kind.

"The boom will knock you overboard," he warned as I protested that I didn't want to go down into that smelly place. When I saw the boom sweep across the boat as we came about, I figured I'd better do as he said. Reluctantly, I climbed down into the cabin, holding my breath to keep from losing my supper.

We made it safely to Cambridge where Bob sold the oysters to J.M. Bramble's packing house. We made light of all the drama of the storm. That night, we walked uptown through the quiet streets of Cambridge, a small town, mostly watermen, a few stores and businesses. We window shopped and dreamed of the day when we could afford all the wealth in the windows: jewelry, clothes and furniture. Sometimes, when we journeyed to Cambridge, we splurged and spent the night at the De Cater House for five dollars a night.

Sailing home in the morning after a storm took your breath away. The Bay spanned out, splendid and calm, making it hard to remember the furious waters of the night before. Dazzling mornings like that taught me a love of the water and erased my fears. I loved to stand on the deck in early dawn as the sun rose above the horizon. I'll never forget the scene I took in: fresh air blowing so crisply, the trees on the shore beginning to lose their leaves of scarlet and gold, and overhead, the honking of wild geese as they slowly rose into the air winging their way southward.

Bob stood with one arm around my shoulders, the other on the wheel. He looked so much like a little boy, smiling down at me, his hair tousled from the breeze. He whispered in my ear, "Aren't you glad you came with me, little powder puff?" he said. That was my nickname when I was on the boat because he said I was so little the wind would whisk me away like a powder puff.

"I didn't think the world could be so quiet and misty," I said, watching the clouds of fog rise, covering the sun in spots. The cool air brushed my cheeks and I felt the chill of winter.

"It's Indian Summer now," Bob said. "Let's enjoy it while it lasts. Stay up on deck with me. Who wants breakfast anyway?"

That suited me just fine. I wasn't looking forward to cooking in the smelly old cabin.

We sat down together and watched the rippling waves wash against the boat. "Let's just sail off into the ocean and forget the world, just you and me," I said.

"Come on you dreamer," Bob chided me. "When we get old, we can dream. Now we have to work." Accepting the truth of what he said, I gave him a kiss and walked to the end of the boat.

November was always Oyster Supper time on the Island. The churches held their annual suppers when oysters were plentiful and the farms had harvested their crops. It seemed that traditions of the Island people kept popping up which I knew nothing about! After the first year full of surprises, I think I was ready for anything!

First, we had to collect for the oyster supper. Myrtle Kapisak stopped by while I was washing dishes one evening to ask if I wanted to go with her the next day to collect. Bob was digging sweet potatoes and raised no objections when I asked if he could spare me the following day. He presented me with a handful of bright gold sweet potatoes to give to Myrtle. The smell of freshly dug earth clung to them. I knew Myrtle would appreciate the gift. When Bob had finished digging the potatoes and had piled them all in the yard to dry, he came in to wash his hands before going to pump the boat out.

"I have never asked anyone for anything before," I told him, "How will I know what to say?"

"The girls do it every year," he said. "Don't worry, they'll show you the ropes."

The next morning Myrtle and Anna arrived at 8:00, signalling me with the car's horn. I grabbed my sweater, left Bob to cook supper, and joined them in the car. The three of us sat in front because chicken coops filled the back seat and the trunk.

"Let's hope we get them all filled by 4:00," said Myrtle.

"We will," Anna replied. "We always do."

We drove to all the nearby farms and communities. Everywhere, people poured out their hearts in giving. Farmers gave live chickens, eggs, canned goods, pickles, jellies and potatoes. If the farmer wasn't home, his wife would say, "There are plenty of chickens in the yard if you want to catch a couple." You should have seen us, calling the chickens and flaying our arms in a circle to corner them. One of us would run in the flock and catch one before all of them escaped. Some job, but we always succeeded in getting at least one.

The stores gave sugar, lard and hams. The oyster houses gave oysters by the gallon - already shucked.

I learned then that when a church goes out to work, they really work. I saw so many kind people that day, my heart was touched. I wish there were more of them in the world. A few grouches and stingy-minded people shut the door in our faces. We laughed if off. Like Paul in the Bible, we shook the dust off our feet and praised God for the generous ones.

Afterwards, we prepared all the goodies we had collected. Two days before the supper, we killed, picked and roasted chickens, baked hams and candied sweet potatoes. We made soup from the livers, necks and giblets in a huge pot, then feasted on it for lunch. We made Maryland beaten biscuits with the flour. Bob's Aunt Annie was known as the best biscuit maker in the community. I added patting oysters to my ever-growing repertoire of Island knowledge.

We peeled bushels of potatoes, sliced cabbage, made cakes, pies and ice cream. We had no electric gadgets to assist us. I didn't think so few people could do so much work. Our church had a reputation for hosting the tastiest suppers for miles around.

The suppers were held in the upstairs hall of Mr. Walter Weber's abandoned store. The floors were rough boards and the kitchen stoves stood at one end. There was a curtain to separate the dining room from the cooking area. The tables were set with crisp white tablecloths, ironed and starched to perfection by hand. People came from miles away to enjoy the feast and visit with old friends.

We worked and sweated, deep fried oysters and waited on tables. All the food was served family style, giving everyone all they wanted to eat for $2.50. The suppers were held for two nights and we auctioned off the leftovers. Usually we made about $300, a decent profit at the time.

Cleaning up afterwards was a day's work. All of the church women pitched in to clean the hall for the next season. We carried water up the stairs from Miss Laura's house, heated it on the stove, then washed all the pots and pans. Then the stoves were polished until they shone like glass. We scrubbed the floors on our hands and knees, usually managing to get splinters stuck in our fingers and knees. Working together, we felt a keen sense of accomplishment and heaved a big sigh of relief that all had gone smoothly.

I remember one year Bob had been gone all week. He came home after he loaded his boat with oysters. He had paid all of his money for oysters but five dollars. He gave it to me and said, "Here, honey, is five dollars for our supper, you keep it."

I laid it on the table and finished dressing and forgot all about the money. When we were ready to go out the door, I looked on the table for the five dollars but saw no money. I said, "Bob, did you pick up the money?"

"No," he replied, "I gave it to you."

"Well, it's gone. What do we do now?" I asked.

"Well, I guess we stay home," he answered.

Then it came to me. I picked up some scraps of paper the children left on the table. I must have picked up the money with the papers and threw it all in the stove. Bob was angry with me and I was furious with myself.

"You sure can't be trusted with money," he scoffed.

"I know I'm stupid, but you don't have to rub it in," I sarcastically answered. It almost ended in a fight, but I knew I had to go to the hall to wait on tables, so we silently walked out the door. When it was time for all of us cooks to eat, I said we weren't hungry.

"Not hungry after all this work!" They kept at us until I confessed I had burned our money. Boy did they laugh at me. "Come on, dinner is on us, you can pay next time," they said. That broke the ice between Bob and I.

When Bob told me of the ways of the oyster men, it was a reminder of the excitement of threshing time in the west. The big steam threshing machine went from ranch to ranch with the threshing crew, mostly for a week or two, however large a crop of wheat the rancher had until the threshing was finished.

I loved to watch the big black steam engine pull into the field. The men wore red bandannas across their faces to keep the swirling chaff from choking them. I watched with awe as the golden wheat was pitched into the thresher from the wagons of wheat. The wheat binder had already cut and bound the wheat into bundles. Now the thresher separated the wheat from the straw. It was fascinating to watch the wheat pour out of the pipe. Two men stood by with gunny sacks directly under the pipe to catch the wheat. As the bags were filled, two other men were there to tie the bags. If the rancher had a silo, the wheat was blown directly into the silo where it was kept waiting for a good market.

Our kitchen was full of supplies like the oyster boats. Homebaked pies, cakes, roasted chicken and beef each day. We girls helped with the work and waiting on tables. At night, the men slept in the bunkhouse. Before bedtime, they sat around the campfire singing and playing cowboy songs. Mother let us listen for a while, then off to bed, but the music drifted through the windows and put us to sleep.

One summer, Dad didn't have time to go to Lewistown to buy supplies so he sent me on horseback to town. I saddled Goldie and started out in the morning with my list of groceries.

Dad said, "Be sure you have them all tied on before you leave, honey."

"Sure, Dad," I yelled back as I trotted off. It was hot and the road was dusty. I stopped for Goldie to take a long drink of cool water as I crossed over Spring Creek. I dipped my hands and drank from the refreshing water. The sun was hot overhead and I had to hurry. I stopped at Powell's General Store and gave the grocery man the list. He soon had my supplies tied in a gunny sack on the back of my saddle. He sure didn't do much of a job, for by the time I was halfway home, it had slid to one side and all of the groceries were popping out two at a time. Goldie didn't think much of this and neither did I. I stopped to pick up the cans of milk and a bag of sugar that had fallen on the ground when I saw a buckboard behind me, an older gentlemen dressed in western style. A lock of grey hair hung over one eye, his stetson placed in a rakish angle pushed back the rest of his hair. He tipped his hat and drawled in a western manner.

"Young lady, can I help you?"

I was near tears trying to tie everything back on the saddle. He deftly picked up the groceries, tied the bag securely to the saddle, then helped me up on Goldie, tipped his hat again and was gone so quickly, I hardly had time to thank him.

Soon I was home with my bundle of groceries. Dad was worried and waiting for me. The sun was setting in a big ball of fire as I unsaddled Goldie. Mother called me to supper, asking what made me so late.

"Oh, nothing," I tried to brush it off, afraid Dad wouldn't let me go again. I felt so big, going all by myself.

Twilight

So many years have passed, yet memory
    can retain.
The happy days of former years, and friends
    thru joy and pain.
Walk with me along the island shore,
I'll tell you of my home where
    I have lived before.
Gaze far out across the harbor,
there must be fifty ships or more.
From sun to sun the crew must work,
to dredge the oysters from the bay,
then drop their sails and anchor fast,
their work well done at close of day.
Twilight falls, the air is crisp and clear,
the lamps are lit within the homes,
where crackling fires, and children play,
and a stranger welcomed, from where
    he roams.
The school house is a place of joy
where friends and neighbors meet,
to hear their children speak and sing.
to vie for honors, then retreat.
It's Sunday on the island shore,
labored hours and trials are past.
The church bells ring their hour of prayer,
at his feet their burdens cast.
So if some day you chance to wander
down on the Eastern Shore,
find this place of rest,
it will fill your heart with love and joy,
and God will do the rest

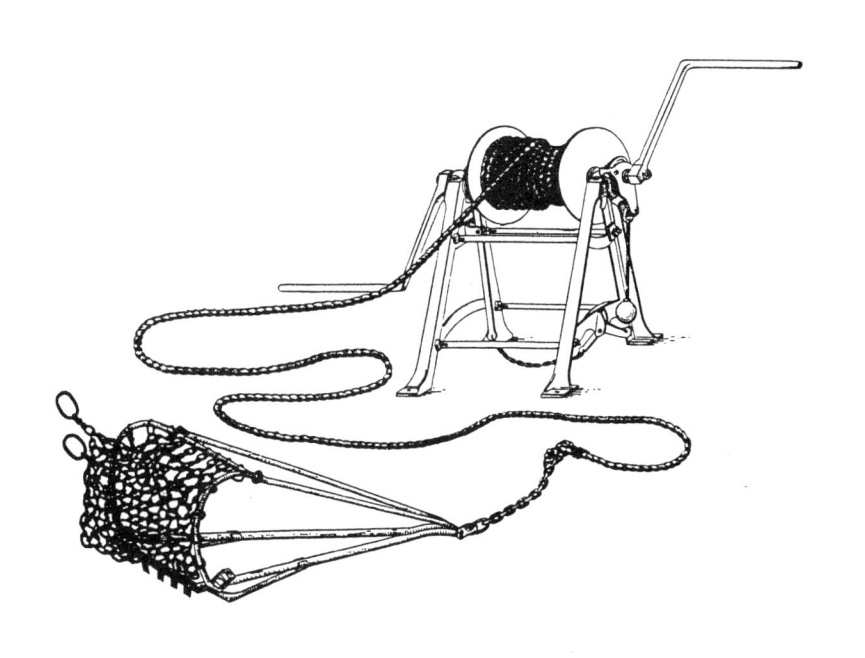

**Oyster dredge and pulley.
(Courtesy of Gorman Cummings.)**

Boats at Faulkner House, Fairbank, Md.

Dredge boats in the harbor, probably about 1920.
(Courtesy Gorman Cummings.)

Black Walnut Cove
(Courtesy of Gorman Cummings.)

Dredging oysters through holes cut in ice.
(Courtesy of Gorman Cummings.)

Car going out on river with empty sleigh and boat
to be loaded with oysters. (Courtesy of Gorman Cummings.)

9

Christmas

Island life wasn't all hard work. Just living in the community proved to be an adventure. Christmas was a special occasion. Everyone prepared fruitcake a month before Christmas. I had to learn that too because Mother had always made cookies and plum pudding. Aunt Annie gave me her recipe for fruitcake. With her help and help from the neighbors, I tentatively baked my first fruitcakes. I packed them in lard cans and was supposed to pour whiskey or rum over them to keep them moist. We kept no liquor in our house, so I used apples, as I had seen Mother use.

Making root beer was another new experience for me. It was made in a lard can, then bottled and set by the fire to ripen. Everybody's house looked like a distillery, but it sure tasted good. As far as I can remember, the recipe called for one bottle of root beer essence, five pounds of sugar, two yeast cakes and enough water to fill the can.

A week before Christmas, I made four or five more cakes: black walnut, chocolate, orange and fresh coconut. I scarcely had any fingers left after grating the coconut! I made Bob's most prized cake, a Minnie HaHa cake, which had four layers and was frosted with dried fruit, coconut, nuts, cherries and raisins. A sugar syrup was boiled until it spun a thread, then poured over the fruit. This was spread between the layers and on top of the cakes. Your eyes tasted it before your mouth did!

Two days before Christmas, a farmer came by selling turkeys and chickens. He knocked on the door and when I opened it, he tipped his hat, "Marm, I have chickens and turkeys for sale," he said. For five dollars, I bought a turkey, which had to be killed.

"Bring me a gunney sack," he said. I rummaged around until I found a potato sack and handed it over, wondering what he was going to do with it. He soon showed me.

He cut a hole in the bottom of the bag, tied the bag to the clothesline and put Mr. Turkey inside with his head out the hole. With a quick slash of his knife, he slit his throat and tied the turkey on the line to bleed.

When Bob came home, he cut it down and brought it into the house. We saved the wings for a feather duster. We dipped the turkey in boiling water; my, what a stench and what a job! Eventually Mr. Turkey was clean as a whistle, ready to be roasted to a crisp golden brown for Christmas dinner.

Since this was my first Christmas away from home, I felt so homesick thinking of my family making their traditional preparations. Bob and I had only five dollars to our name. We had to make a lark of it, otherwise we would have felt sorry for ourselves. Bob had a boatload of oysters, with our money tied up after paying for the oysters.

"Grab your coat, honey," said Bob. "Let's walk to Tilghman to buy ourselves a present." Off we went again on one of his crazy larks. What else were we to do on Christmas Eve?

We walked out into the crusted snow. It was so deep that Bob walked ahead to make tracks for me. A full moon shone overhead into the dark starry night. The crisp, clear air wasn't really too cold. We stood still for a moment and looked at the North Star, wondering if it was the star that led the shepherds to Bethlehem. "We can imagine it was," said Bob, "and we must hurry or it'll be Christmas before we get there."

At Tilghman, we stomped the snow from our feet and walked into Elmer's Store, the only store that sold dishes and lamps. The big stove in the middle of the room invited us to walk over and warm our hands. I looked around at the conglomeration of everything imaginable, but saw nothing that I considered to be a necessity. I was getting discouraged when my eyes fell on a beautiful Rayo lamp, just what we needed. I pointed it out to Bob who gingerly picked up the price tag. "Five dollars," he almost shouted with glee, and handed the money over to Elmer, who wrapped the lamp carefully so the shade wouldn't break. We walked out of the store, proud as peacocks with our precious bundle.

We had only candles to light our tree. We placed the lamp underneath and the flickering candles shone like stars. We sat by the fire and quietly watched the candles burn down. Our first tree and our first gift glows like a shining light in my memory.

Christmas night was a night of wonder for all the Island. We prepared our church program feverishly for weeks. We trained the children for their parts and decorated the church. We fashioned a large welcome sign of Christmas greens and strung it across the platform. People from all the churches crowded into the tiny chapel. Since the church had electricity, the tree was ablaze with lights. Everyone took part in the program of plays and songs. The children recited their pieces. Bob's sisters, Myrtle and Mildred, sang a duet and his younger sister, Josephine, sang a lullaby to the baby Jesus cradled in a bed of straw.

Suddenly there was a ringing of sleigh bells. Santa burst into the room and placed his pack on the floor while all the children gathered around, each taking a gift and clapping their hands in glee. They watched him as he sang a song of good cheer and waved a hearty good night. Then he vanished, his sleigh bells echoing in the night air.

The congregation joined in singing "Oh Come All Ye Faithful." Parting with enthusiastic wishes for a Merry Christmas, they walked out into the night, carrying their sleeping babies home. We rejoiced in our simple program, prepared by loving hands, our gift to God for His Son.

During Christmas week, each family visited their neighbors bearing Christmas cheer, filling one another's homes with joy. By the end of the week, our parties successfully consumed most of my cakes and our homemade root beer.

Christmas

The magic glow of Christmas
Comes stealing through the air;
It's wafted on the morning breeze,
It breathes an evening prayer.
Again it tells the age-old story
Of a bright and shining star,
Which led the wise men and the shepherds,
From their flocks and fields afar.
It falls upon the young and old,
A child's enchanted face.
It gleams within the firelight's glow,
Which shelters every race.
Each year it comes to bring us hope,
To guide us through the days of stress.
Each year it leaves a brighter glow,
For warmth and happiness.

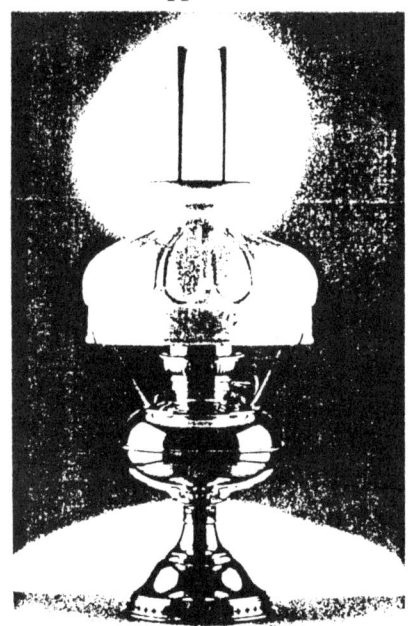

Rayo Lamp
(Photography by Ken Bell.)

Christmas Tree and Rayo Lamp
(Picture painted by Cindy Fletcher.)

10

Springtime on the Island

The dredging season ended in January. The men anchored the dredge boats in the cove to be repaired and to await the next season. The busy month of February followed, full of preparations for pound net fishing in the spring.

The snow was melting in spots and the ice flows slowly made their way out of the harbor into the Bay. It was still windy and cold, but some spring days were warm and the sun felt hot for a few hours. Here and there you could see tiny twigs longing to burst out with leaves. The geese were honking overhead, flying north for their nesting grounds. Even with the cold winds, you felt the stir of spring, knowing that soon the first robins, the harbinger of spring, would be running over the ground looking for the twigs to make their nests.

Captain Bain's net house was located in his back yard. I accepted Bob's invitation to join him while he was working in the net house one day. I smelled the tar before I entered and held my nose. I walked in gingerly, stepping around the messy piles of nets on the floor. Hesitating for a moment, I sat down beside Bob on the floor because there was no place else to sit. The overwhelming tar smell quickly forced me to abandon him to continue his work alone.

"Bye, honey, I don't like your tar! I'll see you after a while," I said.

"Coward!" he quipped back at me.

As far as I can remember, the nets are dragged out of the net house in separate piles, spread on the ground and repaired. Then they are placed in pots of boiling tar. This is to preserve and keep the nets from tearing. They are again spread out on the ground to dry. The first day Bob came home, his face and arms had angry red blisters from the tar and sun.

Running water was unheard of and no one had showers. He splashed cold water from the pump all over his face and then bathed in the wash tub. I had to laugh because with all the vigorous scrubbing, he looked like a big, red lobster. He returned to his normal color in a few days.

The next step was for the men to load the pound net piles onto a barge and tow them to the fishing grounds. Everyone coveted Captain Bain's fishing grounds because the fish were so plentiful there. The pound net poles were sunk into the bottom of the Bay by hand: a horrible, back-breaking job. Later, the men jacked the poles down with power. As I continually witnessed, even with the onset of power-operated machinery, the waterman led a tedious, day-by-day job, requiring guts, muscle and determination. They seemed to accept their life as it was, and were happy and fulfilled with each passing season.

By March, the men had readied the nets to be tied to the poles. They placed the nets so that the trap was in a "leader", which closed the trap to keep the fish inside. The next day, the men returned with hand dip nets to remove the fish from the nets and put them into the waiting boats. They took the fish to the fish houses to be packed for market. Captain Bain always sold his fish to Captain Burt Faulkner, who owned one of the largest packing houses on Tilghman.

I learned how to bake shad and rock fish. We didn't serve herring much because it had too many bones, but Bob did cut the roe out. We enjoyed eating it fried. I canned some herring roe as well.

Spring came. I saw my family for the first time since our wedding. Mother and Dad came to visit us for a few days. Ione and Howard with their children came from New York. Jennie and Leslie visited and brought their baby boy, Sherman. Minibel came on her spring vacation from the teacher's college in Salisbury she was attending. Floyd and his wife Edith drove down on Sunday with their five children. We enjoyed a real family reunion, a time for all of us to rejoice and be happy.

Unfortunately, I felt depressed for days after they left. I devoted myself to writing lengthy letters, the only form of contact. Each week I waited eagerly for letters with news from home. Mother never failed me as always. At the end of each letter, she closed with a little spiritual thought for the day, a Bible verse.

I kept busy planting the hundred strawberry plants that Dad generously brought us for our garden. We threw all of our energy into planting the rest of the garden. Bob hired a mule from Mr. Fairbanks to plow and work the ground as usual.

The church held a strawberry festival in the church yard. With white covered tables and chairs, it looked like a banquet. Everyone brought food and this soon turned into one big picnic to raise money for the church. We had it early in the afternoon before the mosquitoes came out to devour us.

Afterward, the tablecloths were taken home to be washed, ironed and put away for the fall oyster suppers.

Housewives kept busy during the spring. We cleaned the house from top to bottom. I papered and painted all of our rooms, skills my Dad had taught me. He was an expert. Bob got to be quite a skilled paper hanger and worked diligently helping me. Everyone painted and papered their rooms every spring and fall. We took the windows out and washed them. If panes were loose, we puttied them in and painted the putty to keep it from breaking.

Everyone took their curtains down during the summer to keep the wind from blowing them to pieces. I took mine down too, even though I wasn't used to the windows looking so bare. I put up side drapes to give more charm to the room. We washed the curtains, stacked them and pinned them on curtain stretchers. I never could get mine on straight unless Mother was there to help me. Bob was no good at that.

Since vacuums were not in use, spring and fall found every clothesline draped with blankets, carpets and curtains. We beat the rugs to death with a broom as they hung over the line. In later years, Bob bought me a vacuum. What a joy! I don't think there was a house in Fairbank that wasn't so clean you could eat off the floor.

We took down all the beds, washed them and put them back together. My mother told me when she was a girl, you took a feather duster dipped in coal oil and cleaned all the cracks after the beds had been washed. If some bedbug was hiding there from a stranger's sleeping in your bed, the intruder's life was put to an end. This sounded funny to me because I had never seen such a bug.

The church also needed a thorough cleaning, so we all pitched in with our mops, polish and dust cloths. We had to haul the water from Miss Laura's. We washed the windows, scrubbed the floors and polished the pews. It took two days, but it was fun and a lot of hard work. We were like the seven dwarfs, singing and whistling in unison.

Bob and Lloyd pound net fishing.

Pulling in the anchor.

Pulling in net.

Distributing the load is Robert Bradshaw.

Boat entering pound net to load fish.

Bob and his brother, Lloyd, pulling in the net and anchor filled with fish.

11

Our Halloween Party

October arrived. The air grew chilly. Occasionally a few snow flakes floated off into space. I watched the wild geese winging their way southward again, and I walked down to the wharf to enjoy the spectacular sunset. Across Black Walnut Cove, the trees swayed in the breeze, showing off their fall colors of green and gold. A lone leaf fell at my feet. I picked it up and gently touched the delicate veins, marveling at how beautifully it was made. I wondered at God's creation, how everything could be so perfect. The sun's rays shone on the water in sparkling colors. I saw it sinking behind the trees now, shades of deep red and gold. The geese gracefully swooped down in the open field in a slow honking sound of contentment for the night.

The gentle lap of the waves washing up on the shore woke me from my reverie. A row boat slowly approached. Captain Earn Jenkins and Moni rowed up to the wharf, tied their boat and stepped out.

"Looks like a nor'easter coming up with those storm clouds approaching," said Captain Jenkins. "Alice, what are you doing down here?"

I usually relished the peaceful shore while I waited for Bob. Captain Earn chewed tobacco and had a big wad in his cheek. I stepped back as he spit to keep the juice from splattering all over my feet. As they walked away, I saw Bob rowing ashore with his sister, Josephine.

Jo ran home to get permission to have supper with us. While I was cooking dinner, I thought how nice it would be to have a Halloween party and invite all the neighbors. Immediately, Jo got excited and we began hatching a plan. Bob balked at the idea, but finally agreed. Sitting at the table after dinner, Jo and I made a guest list. We started making decorations the very next day because Halloween was only two weeks away.

I transformed our living room into a spooky witch's den with skeletons, bats and old sheets hung over the furniture. One of my cooking pots, covered with black crepe paper, became a cauldron. One of the guests dressed up as a witch. I wrote fortunes for everyone, and they all fished them out of the pot. Bob brought home a chain from the boat. I put it by the door and it rattled noisily when people entered.

The big night finally arrived and I think the whole island was in masquerade. The guests were dressed as skeletons, witches and black cats. We played games, then turned off the lights and told ghost stories. I served orange punch. I had made an intricate spider web on the Devil's food cake. We roared with laughter and everyone declared it was the best party ever. People remembered it for years.

Sometime that summer I discovered I was pregnant. I wasn't sure how Bob felt, although we had both talked of children. I hesitated to tell him the good news for I knew he loved to have me on the boat with him, and this would end our trips together. Finally I gathered enough courage to tell him. I was so excited myself that I couldn't wait another minute.

After the party we sat down to relax with a cup of coffee. Bob looked at me and said, "That was sure a humdinger of a party, honey! You must be bushed; in fact, you look tired."

I sipped my coffee and thought it was the right time. "You know, I am a little tired. Let's just sit for a few minutes and clean up later. I have something to tell you." I still hesitated and gulped my last bit of coffee. "You know why I am tired?"

"Because you have worked for a week getting ready for the party! I told you to get yourself up to bed and I'll clean up."

"No, it wasn't the party, honey, I'm pregnant!" I exclaimed.

"You're what?" He looked at me in astonishment. It took a few minutes for my words to sink in. I was holding my breath when he jumped up and yelled, "Whoa! Are you really, honey, you're not kidding?"

The next minute he calmed down and picked me up and started for the stairs. "You're going to bed, young lady, right now." When I finally got a word in, I protested but to no avail. I was going to bed.

In the morning, the wind was blowing a gale. That meant the dredgers wouldn't be working unless the wind calmed down. Bob stayed home with me. All he talked about was the baby. I couldn't even put my foot on the boat for a long time. He was thinking of when his mother fell and he was concerned that I be very careful.

I assured him that I'd be fine and we had a great day together making plans for the baby.

12

My Father's Death

The next night, I had a terrific pain in my right side. For a week, I suffered with it. Finally, Bob said I had to see our family doctor, Dr. Palmer, in Easton. He borrowed his father's car for the trip. Dr. Palmer diagnosed it right away as appendicitis and wanted to operate immediately.

Since I was three months pregnant, I was afraid of the operation. The doctor insisted that if I waited and had an attack, it would be worse for me. Bob and I decided to heed his advice. I returned to the Island for the weekend to pack my clothes, going through each room in the house as if I wouldn't see it again. I tried not to show Bob my fear, but I'm sure he felt it.

Monday morning, November 5, I had the operation. Much to my surprise, everything went smoothly, but the doctor kept me in bed for ten days. Mother sent me little gifts and Dad took trips out to be with me. Bob was running oysters and couldn't make it to the hospital every day.

It was cold and snowing when I left the hospital. The doctor said that I couldn't walk upstairs, so Mother insisted that I stay with her and Dad. Bob was in Cambridge, so Dad took me home. The next day, he came down with pneumonia. There were no miracle drugs for pneumonia in those days and Dad got worse. We called Dr. Palmer but he didn't give us much hope because Dad's heart was weak.

A week before Christmas, December 17, 1927, Dad passed away. My family was overwrought with sadness at his death. I was thankful to be home with Mother for a few days as she felt completely overwhelmed.

My Dad was very special to me. I treasured the many memories of sitting by the fire as a young girl and talking with him. I remember him as a very wise person, worthy of my respect.

Running a farm was a difficult and demanding way of life. Mother couldn't manage it all herself and eventually sold the farm. She and Minibel made a home together. She visited all of us sometime during the year. Bob and I enjoyed her visits tremendously. She gave me her piano and spent many hours at the piano playing and singing.

Mother and I became much closer once Dad was gone. We had never taken much time to sit and visit with each other. She told me stories of her childhood.

Her father, Robert P. Sheldon, was a Methodist minister. My grandmother and grandfather met at a Revival Service. Grandmother was twenty-seven and Grandfather was forty-eight. It was love at first sight. They were married the same year. Grandfather was a circuit rider traveling many miles through forests where there were no roads. Later he was commissioned by the U.S. Government to teach and preach on the Rosebud Indian Reservation near Mt. Pleasant, Michigan.

They raised their family here until Mother was eight. When they left the Reservation, Mother had a hard time adjusting to life with other white people. She was afraid of them. When she left, she took an Indian Doll with her that her Indian playmate gave her. It seemed to comfort her when she was afraid at night.

Mother told me a funny story about Grandmother. Apparently, one time she hung her freshly ironed white clothes in the storage room. Suddenly, the clothes moved! She panicked because behind them she saw an Indian. Not knowing what to do, Grandmother screamed and ran out of the house. The Indian followed right behind her and the faster she ran, the faster he ran. Finally, she fell and the Indian caught her. He leaned over and picked her up even though she was still screaming. Grandfather heard her cries and came running. The Indian handed her over and said "Me no hurt white squaw. Me look at white clothes." After this incident, the Indian, Nar-a-gas-ick, became a close friend of the family and visited them long after they left the Reservation. He would come at night and rock us to sleep when we were children.

Mother and Dad married in 1893. In the spring of 1909, Mother's doctor warned her that the winters in Mt. Pleasant, Michigan were ruining her health. He recommended that Dad take her west where she could breath fresh, dry air.

The government was giving away homestead land to settlers willing to build upon it. After seven years, the settlers earned the right to own the land. Dad and my oldest brother, Floyd, who was 14, went west to find a homestead and build a home in Lewistown, Montana.

Dad returned telling of the house he and neighbors had built. Its bay window overlooked the "Little Rockies", mountains that were snowcapped all summer. As Dad talked of the land out west, Mother fully realized for the first time that she would be leaving everything she had ever known.

"It's beautiful," my father told her. "It's 4,000 feet high and you feel like you can almost reach heaven."

He brought us beautiful gifts: a white lace embroidered shirt waist for Ione, a red plaid one for Mama (Which Papa said would show off her beautiful eyes); a hand embroidered sewing box from the Orient for Susie; a cowboy hat for Jennie; a cowgirl dress for Minibel and a big teddy bear for me.

We sold the farm, and everything on it at auction. Dad kept only enough furniture and farm implements to start our new life. He loaded it on a box car and freighted it West. Mother kept her organ. A photographer took a picture of the family standing on the veranda one final time before the big move.

We donned our best clothes for the trip west on the train, and crossed Lake Michigan by steamer, then took the Great Union Pacific across the prairies and through the mountains to Montana, known by the Indians as the "Land of Shining Mountains."

The River Wedding

Just imagine if you can
The deep dark forests of Michigan.
On the river bank there stood a house
Where lived a Preacher and his spouse.
Travelers passing on this trail
Found no bridge with a rail.
Just a ford where they must dash
Through the water with a splash.
One morn in early spring
When all the world did sing.
And the river rushing by
Was so swift and high
The Preacher heard a shout
And saw as he went out
A couple on the other side
Wishing to be tied.
The water rushing by was swift and high
And the bride began to cry.
In those days a license you did not need
Before with a marriage you could proceed.
The Preacher scratched his head
And "Wait a minute" he said
And disappeared into the house.
But returned with his daughter and his spouse
With slicked down hair
And aprons tossed on a chair.
For at every wedding there must be
Two witnesses there to see.
And above the roaring water soon was heard
"Do you take this woman as your bride?"
"I do," came from the other side.
"Then I pronounce you Man and Wife.
And wish you happiness all your life."

By lone Butler Hunt

Frank and Allie Butler.

Ranch house (Montana) Bar $\overline{63}$.

Alice and Minibel.

Mt. Pleasant, Michigan. Our farm house with the family on the porch.
Lower front: Mother and Dad Left: Ione, Minibel, Jennie, Alice, Susie, Curlo our dog, Floyd on Kit.

13

Our First Child

The following spring came early after winter's ice storms that broke electric lines from the falling ice-laden tree branches. Even roads were blocked and warnings rang out over the radio to stay off the highways as trees and electric wires were falling. It was not safe. The open fields looked like frozen lakes. a beautiful crystal fairyland to look at but treacherous to drive.

April was a month of beauty with the pussy willows pushing up through the March grass, nodding their brown spears with the wind. You welcomed every blade of grass and dandelion that popped up over night. The joy of the spring gave you an elation of new life and hope.

Our son, Robert Reed, was born in the midst of this beauty on April 19, 1928. His birth brought joy and laughter into our lives. Mother was there to welcome him into our lives with Dr. Reeser. Lucy Presson gave him his first bath and from that time on, she was Aunt Lucy to all of our children. All babies were born at home, and I had the joy of being waited on for ten days, for that was the length of time all mothers stayed in bed to cuddle and spoil the baby.

During the winter days before his birth, I was busy shaping a piece of wire into an arch for a canopy over the crib, but it was too much for me. When Bob came in, he wanted to give it a try. In a few minutes he had constructed it into a perfect arch. After I covered it with white dotted swiss fabric, I thought it was an achievement of art, since we had no pattern! I learned alot about crocheting laboring over a pattern for an afghan. I think I spent more time unraveling than I did actually crocheting.

Mother stayed with us for a month, then she was back to her job of nursing other people who needed her.

Reed was a healthy baby of nine months when he contracted double pneumonia. When we called Dr. Reeser, his first orders were to open the windows and keep the stove red hot. Then apply an onion poultice. I was flabbergasted and just looked at him.

"Don't just stand there, get busy!" he ordered.

"What is an onion poultice?" I gasped.

He glared at me as though I was plain dumb, which I guess I was. "Cut up some onions, cook them, and place them in a cloth bag, then place them on the baby's chest," he said.

I grabbed a paring knife and began cutting onions. With tears in my eyes from the onions, I finally found the iron skillet and cooked the onions. Somewhere I found a piece of cloth for a bag. Just then, Theresa Cummings, a neighbor, came in the door. She saw me clumsily trying to wipe the tears away and put the onions in the bag. She knew all these things that were new to me.

"Let me do it, Alice, you look like you're ready to collapse." She saw the tears running down my face from the onions and probably thought I was a big baby. I was glad to sit down and watch. Different neighbors came in each night to sit and keep the poultice hot. Although the house smelled like an onion factory, it must have worked for, with our prayers, the onions and neighbors, Reed was up jumping all over his crib in just a few days.

In the early spring of 1929, Mrs. Bradshaw's health began to fail. Her paralysis had weakened her heart until she was totally confined to her bed. She needed constant care. It was difficult for Captain Bain, for he was preparing his nets for pound net fishing, so Bob and Lloyd did most of the work that year, with the help of the crew.

The girls were good nurses in caring for their mother, but her condition gradually grew worse, until on April 2, 1929 she passed away. It was a trying time for the family to adjust without their mother; even though she had been paralyzed for many years, her presence had been there to give her warmth and love to them. Their task was finished and their mother gone from the home. With their father's help, they worked together to mend their sorrow and make a happy home.

Bob especially missed his mother sitting in the window waving to him each morning as he passed the house going to work.

Mrs. Bradshaw was born in Fruitland, Maryland on Jan. 19, 1860. Her maiden name was Richardson. She had a sister, Emma, and several half-brothers. After she and Captain Bain were married, they lived on Holland Island where five of their children were born, before moving to Fairbank.

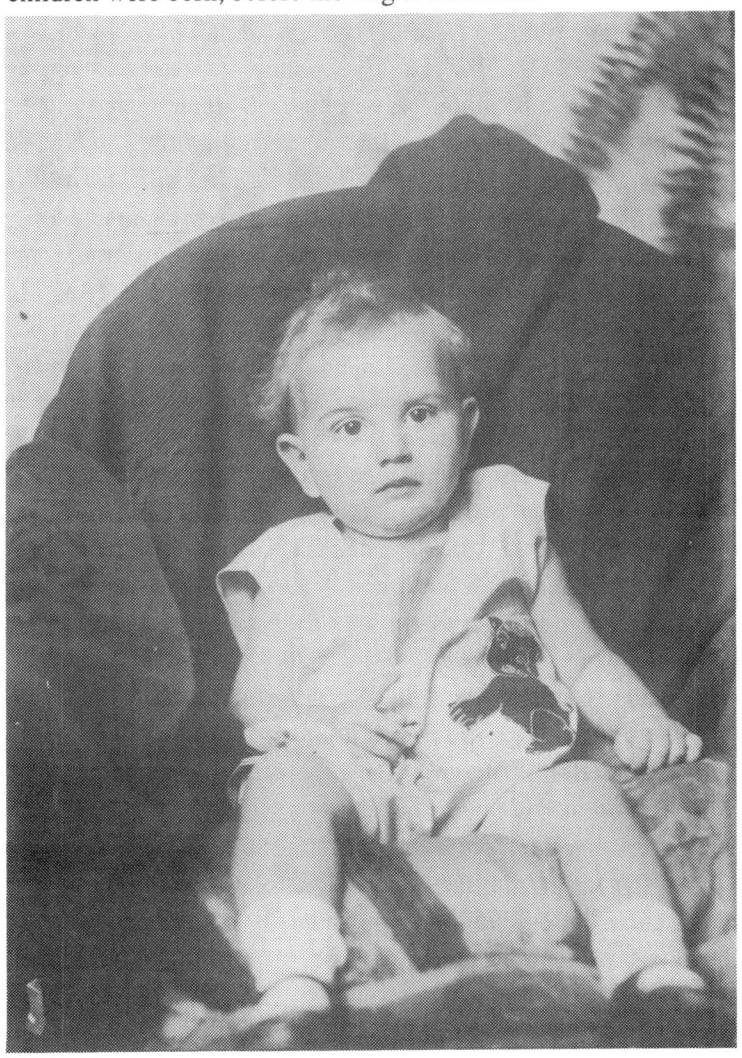

Robert Reed Bradshaw - first picture.

14

Lady Alice

Bob longed for a boat of his own. We didn't have the money so he cashed in his life insurance policy, worth one thousand dollars, to have a boat built. It was built of wood, thirty-two feet long with a Palmer engine by Jones Boatyard (Pot-Pie) in Whitman, a small town near Tilghman. He built an awning frame himself and I sewed the canvas on my sewing machine.

When she was all built, Bob came home and grabbed my arm. "Come on. You have to nail her name on the bow," he urged me. "You have to do something if you want to ride in her."

I picked up the baby and together we walked to the shore. There she was, rocking in the wind, her white sides gleaming in the sunlight. She was a beauty.

I gathered up the hammer, nails and aluminum letters. With Bob's help, I drew a straight line to guide me in placing the letters. One-by-one, the letters spelled out her name, "Lady Alice."

With that job done, we went aboard for Bob to take us for our first ride in our very own boat. Bob started her engine and soon we were gliding out of the harbor. We were filled with pride and joy to have a boat of our very own, at last.

The crabs were more plentiful on the Western Shore. With a larger boat, Bob could cross the Bay at dawn and be home by mid-afternoon. He spent the rest of the day until suppertime baiting his lines and preparing for the next day. After supper, he joined the rest of the men at Faulkner's store to talk and joke until about nine when bedtime came. Bob rose too early for breakfast so I packed him enough food for breakfast and lunch. The daily routine began again.

Eight or ten barrels of crabs was a good day's work. That sounds like a lot of crabs, but at two or three dollars a barrel which had to cover gasoline, bait and other expenses, there wasn't much left. Even so, we were happy with our life. We were our own bosses.

When the Bay froze over, all the dredging stopped until the spring thaw. If we were lucky, we had saved enough money from crabbing to last through the bad times, but if not, Tom Faulkner always gave credit.

Even when it was frozen, the Bay was a source of food. Some of the men cut holes in the ice for fishing. Captain Bain salted fish caught in the summer. He was always there to help others. I made fish cakes for breakfast instead of bacon or ham. We also bought salt cod from the store. I made cod fish cakes and fish stew with onions and potatoes for supper. It is amazing how you learn to make so many things out of a small supply.

My grandson Rick asked me once, "How is it, Grandma, when I look in the ice box, there's not much of anything there? Then, before you know it, there's a big meal on the table."

I smiled. "When you learn to get along the way I did," I told him, "a little bit means a lot if you know how to use it."

Mr. Sinclair, our milkman, brought fresh milk to everyone's door. We cooked with evaporated milk. The fresh milk was for the children.

When there was a death in the village, it was customary for friends and neighbors to stop by and supply food for the home. Someone always sat up at night so the family could sleep; as the body was kept at home until the funeral. This was a new experience for me, but I was willing to help. There was no air conditioning and in the summer, we were asked to enter the room several times to lay wet cloths on the face to keep it from turning dark.

One night when I was in the room, the wind blew the door shut, leaving me all alone. Death was an awesome thing to me. Not taking my eyes off the body, I backed to the door and managed to find the knob and slip out. From then on, I was careful not to be the last one in the room.

Miss Laura and Captain Laury Faulkner kept a boarding house for years. They were Tom Faulkner's parents. Captain

Laury had a large garden that he worked from early dawn until noon. He returned in the evening when it was cooler to work again. Anytime you walked down the road at dawn or sunset, he was attacking the weeds with his hoe.

Miss Laura was a wonderful cook. She had a large dining room attached to the house where she served meals to hosts of people. The same people returned year after year for weeks or for weekend vacations. The tables were laden down with food served family style. The men went fishing while the ladies slept and enjoyed the large lawn of trees; the smallest breeze from the water kept them cool.

Bob told me that sometimes they had hayrides into the country. You could hear them laughing and playing Miss Laura's player piano far into the night. If they were churchgoing people, they helped to fill our empty pews at church.

Bathing beach at Black Walnut Cove in Fairbank, Maryland.
(Courtesy of Bernard Kaufman.)

Capt. James Lowery Faulkner and Laura Josephine Faulkner.
(Courtesy of Bernard Kaufman.)

Faulkner boarding house.
(Courtesy of Bernard Kaufman.)

Lady Alice and Bob.

Log Canoe owned by James Faulkner won second prize, a silver cup, at Oxford Regatta, July 4, 1871. (Courtesy of Bernard Kaufman.)

15

Prohibition

When the Prohibition Bill was finally passed on December 16, 1921, it changed the whole country. It affected every city, village and town. Some shouted its praises, while others cursed the day it became a law. Stills became the talk of the day and sprang up in any hidden spot, especially the mountain people, where the law could not find them. Bootleg whiskey was moved across the Canadian border on boats and delivered to bootleggers on the shore, then on to private customers. The bootleggers used a signal system from ship to shore. The Federal Agents (Feds as they were called) eventually found them and they were fined and jailed, but as fast as they were out of business, another still started up. The gun battles were fierce. Bootleg whiskey could be bought anywhere. Some that dealt with the business became millionaires, like drugs it was passed from hand to hand.

Fairbank was caught up in turmoil as all places were. One man who delivered the whiskey had customers for miles around. The customers usually came on Saturday nights in all kinds of transportation; trucks, expensive cars, little cars all rolled into Fairbank. There was only one road in and one road out, so what did they do, but park in every available spot they could find, bushes or trees so their cars wouldn't be identified. Most of them spoke in whispers so their voices were not distinguished for fear of police. If any of the villagers met them, no words were exchanged. They passed with their whiskey bottles hidden under their coats. Sometimes the road was so crowded, it was hardly passable.

Several years passed, no one ever disclosed the man's name, but eventually the still where he bought the whiskey was found and destroyed by the police. The Fairbank man was never reported; if this was his way of making a living, it was no one's business. No one was hurt.

In 1934 the Prohibition Bill was repealed. No more booze and no more parked cars, which made the villagers happy. They never liked it but no one squealed on their neighbor. In 1934 the Prohibition Bill was repealed and things became normal once more.

16

The Great Depression

In 1929, the great depression shattered the world as we knew it. Many people, including Bob's father, lost most of their money when the banks closed. Maybe we were lucky we didn't have any money in the bank to lose.

Wages came to about fifteen dollars a week. We stretched our money to buy all of our food, clothes, wood, and coal. We also had to pay our doctor's bills. Fortunately, we had our own chickens and I baked all of our bread. Once a week, I made five loaves of bread to last all week. Vegetables from the garden helped. The Bay furnished oysters, fish, crabs, ducks and geese in season. We weathered the depression without going on welfare.

I also baked for neighbors and different people off the Island. Everyone loved my Parker House rolls. That was the first on the list, then jelly rolls, doughnuts, pies and cake.

One wealthy lady who had bought one of my cakes at our oyster supper said in her southern drawl, "I have eaten cakes all over the world, but yours are the best! Your chocolate icing is divine! You must put 'butta' in it."

"Yes," I said, "I use both butter and cream." It was cooked, instead of icing like most people make. I felt real proud of my cooking. I wished I had a place for a bakery. There was none on the Island. Of course. Bob and the children were happy too, for they got their share of licking the saucepan and the beaters were the best.

I also did some sewing. Lucy Presson made her living sewing. She was a big help to me.

But flower making was what I liked best. They were made from Oriental wood which came from Sears Roebuck. They were the most beautiful handmade flowers I ever saw, not even the silk ones of today could match their beauty. I made flowers for house arrangements and also for people who used them in the cemetery.

I remember one young boy who had just lost his mother, saw my ad in the paper. He came to me with tears in his eyes to ask if I could make some red roses for his mother. Of course, I agreed. I'm sure more love went into those flowers than any I had ever made. When he picked them up, he smiled at me and through his tears he choked, "Mother will love them."

"Yes, dear, I'm sure she will," I replied, and hugged him.

I think the corsages were the most unique gardenias, violets for spring, and poinsettias for Christmas. It was a joy to help with the finances. I worked far into the night sewing for the children and my cooking on Saturday for the baked goods I sold.

The church continued to be our one foundation. It renewed our faith and kept our hearts open for the needs of others. Today when I picture the depression, the starvation and the hardships, I thank God he placed us in a community where we all helped each other.

We learned a lot about economy. Mother's words came back to me when Grandfather preached on the Indian reservation in Michigan: "Trust in the Lord and do good. The Lord will provide." Many times food was scarce, but the Indians brought them freshly-killed game and armloads of hand-woven blankets. The Indians loved Grandfather. They called him Father Sheldon.

Grandfather's salary was about $200 a year from the government and $200 a year from the Methodist conference.

Grandmother was a midwife. Often she went with Grandfather on his circuit rides to deliver a baby. She stayed with the family, washing and cooking until the mother was able to resume her own work.

17

The August Storm

In August 1931, one of the worst storms of the century descended on the coast, leaving destruction of every description in its path. That day left an indelible imprint on the memory of every person who lived through it. The mighty storm smashed harbors, businesses, homes and boats to splinters.

Tilghman was not as badly damaged as places on the coast, but for the men who worked through the day and far into the night to save their boats, it became a night of horror. They lashed their boats together to keep them from being washed into the Bay. Bob worked with the rest of the men throughout the night with only flashlights to guide them. Wind and rain beat at the windows. With every gust, we expected the rain to come crashing through into our house.

Our house was somewhat higher than the road. I watched as the tide slowly, but surely, kept seeping toward the house. The water was two to three feet deep in the road. Fear gripped my heart at this point. I could only watch and pray. I didn't put Reed to bed for fear of having to get him up in a hurry if we had to leave. I made a bed for him on the floor in the parlor. Bob came home about midnight. The men had done all they could do to save their boats, so we weathered the rest of the night together.

In the early dawn, neighbors began coming out of their homes to review the damage. The tide had stopped just in front of our house. Others closer to the wharf had some water, but not enough to damage them. Destruction was all around. Uprooted trees had fallen across the road so that nothing could get through.

The neighborhood children happily splashed through the water, mindless of the severity of the damage. It was "hey day" for them.

The flood affected the whole Eastern Seaboard. Many lives, homes and boats were lost. For those who depended on their boats for their livelihood, it was hard to think about the future. Black Walnut Cove on Tilghman proved to be a very safe harbor. As I remember, only one dredge boat sank in the storm. For the rest, it took a community of love to rebuild, but with each other's help, we did. The storm had helped us to realize once more that God is still the supreme being ruling over all things in the universe.

August storm - 1931.

Dredge boats washed on the shore.

**Wharf Road – Tilghman – After the storm
(Courtesy of Gorman Cummings.)**

18

The Joy of a Daughter

In the spring of 1931, I was three months pregnant. I had worked until noon weeding strawberry plants. After supper, I put Reed to bed. I felt tired after working so hard in the garden and went to bed early. Some time during the night, I woke up and thought I was dying.

Bob called Doctor Reeser. In the meantime, I grabbed a bottle of ammonia to get my breath and put it to my lips without thinking. I probably got no more than a whiff, but when I told Dr. Reeser, he bawled me out with a string of cuss words for which he was famous. "It's a miracle you're still alive," he said. "Throw that bottle away."

He gave me something to calm my nerves and then sat by my bed watching over me. He didn't think I would live through the night. Eventually, I drifted off to sleep and he left. I had damaged my heart and as a result, had to stay in bed all that summer. Bob did most of the work and Mother came to take care of me. With the help of neighbors, God bless them, we made it through a tough time.

On November 5, I gave birth to a beautiful baby girl. Bob said she was so beautiful that her name had to be Angela. I added Barbara to it. In later years, she became Ann, Angie, or Bunny.

Mother came to stay with us again. She had been living with Minibel who was teaching school in Savage, Maryland.

We hired a lady to help with the work. She was good at most things except the cooking. One day she informed Bob that she didn't scrub floors or stairs on her hands and knees. Bob ended up with most of the housework.

Bob and I prayed fervently. I promised God that if he would let me live to raise my children, I would devote the rest of my life to helping others. Finally, through our prayers, I recovered. Although my health has broken down many times, I am eternally grateful for God's answer to our prayers.

On June 29, 1933, Minibel and Walter were married. I was happy for them. They visited us some weekends. Minibel wanted to take Angela so I could rest. She loved children and I knew the baby would be well taken care of. As our family grew, she became like a second mother to all the children. They loved the farm and begged to stay. Walter raised white Leghorn chickens for market as well as farming. The children clamored to gather the eggs. One time Patti was gathering eggs when a rooster chased her. She ran for the house and Minibel threw the broom at the rooster.

Mother had made her home with Minibel until she was married, then she bought a small house in Cambridge which Frank, Minibel's son, called The Dollhouse, because the rooms were so small. Later she sold it and Walter and Minibel made part of the farmhouse over for her. It was very comfortable with a nice sitting room, bath and bedroom. She enjoyed helping with the cooking and canning.

While Mother was living in the Dollhouse, Bob and I often visited for weekends. She loved her grandchildren and was always happy to have us with her. She was a very devout Christian and tried to bring us up in the same manner.

Many nights while Bob was away when I was rocking Angela to sleep, Mother told me more stories of her childhood days on the Reservation. It was hard for me to realize how happy she was after I had read so many horror stories of Indians when we lived in the West.

This is another frightening story Grandmother told me about the time that she and her brothers were left by themselves one day. When Grandmother worked as a midwife, she went to deliver an Indian baby. That day her brothers called her to play with them. Her father used a buffalo horn to call the Indians to church. One of her brothers blew a loud, clear blast on the horn and then told her "Allie, you'd better jump in the apple barrel. The Indians are coming and they will scalp you."

She let them put her in the apple barrel because she was so scared. They put the lid on and ran off to play. She stayed in the barrel, frightened and crying, until her mother came home. When her mother found out what the boys had done, she made them spend the rest of the day splitting wood. Mother's brothers always teased her because she was the only girl.

My grandmother came from Switzerland with her family when she was eight years old. Her mother died when she was born and her father married again. All of her stepsisters treated her like Cinderella. She had to do all the work while they rode in the carriage to spend the day in the country.

The ship they sailed on from Switzerland lost its mast in a storm and was blown off course. They were at sea for three months. During the storm, some of her father's gold which was packed in wooden ferkins (buckets) rolled overboard, so when they arrived they were not only in a strange land, but they had very little money. Her father had been very wealthy, so it was hard for him to adjust to the new and difficult circumstances.

After they landed in New York City, her father left the family in an apartment where they kept a pig on the roof to eat up all the garbage. Grandfather traveled to Ohio, bought one hundred acres for $1000 in 1832 when the Ohio Valley was opened up to immigrants; President Andrew Jackson signed the deed. Sue, our youngest, and I just found the record when we went to Ohio in 1994.

When Grandfather returned, they killed the pig for food and the family traveled to their new home. The house is still standing.

Grandmother was not happy at home, so she learned dressmaking and was hired by families to do all their sewing for one year. Then she traveled to another family. The work was all done by hand, coats, hats, dresses and underwear, also men's suits.

The next spring, April 1932, Jennie became very ill. The doctor diagnosed her problem as an enlargement of the heart. Three days after the birth of her fifth child, she passed away. She had always been such a robust girl, it was hard to believe she was gone. She was a wonderful mother, always doing for others.

She and Leslie lived in Barneck so we visited back and forth a lot. We renewed our childhood days when I wanted everything she did. I fell and broke my arm riding one day when I was small. The first thing she did for me was teach me to write with my left arm so I wouldn't fall back in my lessons. I missed her very much and so did the community.

Angela Barbara Bradshaw (5 years old)

Angela and Reed.

Minibel and Walter Lankford.

19
Company from Michigan

I had never met any of my relatives from Michigan, my home state, since I was only five when our family moved west. I knew my aunts, uncles and cousins in Michigan by name but had never met any of them.

One summer day, a letter came from my cousin, Garnet. She and her sister, Hazel, her husband, Frank, and her niece planned to visit us. I couldn't imagine four people visiting all at one time! Our house wasn't very big. What was I to do?

I stood in the middle of the floor with my hand to my head trying to think. I exclaimed, "What will I do?"

"Honey, it isn't that bad," said Bob with his impish grin. "I'll help with the cleaning and cooking." He did help. We scrubbed the floors, polished the furniture and made up the beds in the children's rooms. The children were happy as larks hearing they could sleep on the floor in the parlor. We worked until midnight to get everything ready before they arrived.

I asked Garnet if they had any trouble finding our house. "We looked for a house with lace curtains," she said, "but nobody had curtains. We thought we were in the wrong community."

"We drove up and down the road looking for a house with lace curtains," said Frank.

"But every place we came to, we said to ourselves that Alice couldn't live there because there were no lace curtains," added Garnet. "Finally we asked a man on the road who pointed out your house." I told her that on the Island, everyone takes their curtains down for the summer.

The unpredictable things children do come back to my mind as I write. In the midst of everything else, Angela took the cake by standing in the middle of the floor and like a little actress with her hand to her head, reenacted my distress the day before. I could have spanked her, but our visitors doubled over with laughter. Remembering the little things that children do seems amusing now, but embarrassing at the time.

We had a wonderful visit and I never panicked again. The more people came, the better time we had. Bob took them fishing one dark rainy night. They had never been out in a storm before. The thunder and lightning panicked them and lashing waves drenched them to the bone. Bob was his cool self and told them not to worry. "The boat is safe," he laughed, but I don't think he convinced them. They stepped ashore gratefully. They came every year after that to see us, but there were no more storms to frighten them and no more panic.

Ione and Howard also came each summer for a week. We had so much fun talking about old times and visiting Walter and Minibel. They had five children, and all the children slept on the floor, with no sleeping bags, just blankets and pillows.

I almost had another disaster when we entertained the minister for Sunday dinner, Reverend McDonald. After I called and invited them I forgot they had thirteen children. Most were grown. Later in the afternoon, Mrs. McDonald called and said there would be only her and the Reverend. I wanted a special dinner, but I didn't have any soup plates. So Bob and I walked to Tilghman and bought a set. All I remember about the dinner was the soup plates.

The ice man was another great thing in those days. No one had refrigerators and so we had to depend on him for ice. He came nearly every day. For a quarter, we could buy enough ice to last two days, unless it was 100 degrees. This was a great treat for the children. They ran to get chips of ice as he picked off the chunks.

Garnet Baskerville, Alice Bradshaw and Hazel Hitz.

Jeanette, Frank and Hazel Hitz, and friend.

20

Bob's Hairy Experience

Sometimes the snow drifts were so deep that the cars couldn't get through the roads. This was one of those winters. Bob was running oysters to Cambridge. It was Christmas Eve, and he hadn't been home for a week. He and Nathan Parks were working together and he had tied up his boat in Cambridge. The ice was so thick that he couldn't come home. I had no Christmas tree or anyone to help me with the children's toys. I thought that this Christmas, the children and I would be celebrating without Bob. Angela was about two years old. She laid out cookies for Santa, then turned to me.

"Mommy, how is Santa going to get through the snow if Daddy can't?"

"Santa has eight reindeer and a sleigh," I told her. "Daddy has a boat that doesn't run through the ice."

"But we don't have a tree," she whimpered as I carried her upstairs to bed.

"Don't worry, Santa can work wonders," I assured her.

Silently, I said a prayer and went back downstairs wondering what I was going to do for the children's Christmas.

As if in answer to my prayer, our neighbor, Bernard Kaufman, came by to see if I needed any firewood.

"Do you think Mr. Bob will be home tonight?" he asked.

I told him my fears that he wouldn't be home. I told him that I was alone with no tree and no one to help put the children's toys together.

He offered to help and together we got to work on the toys. We had nearly finished when the door flew open. Bob stood there grinning with a big, frosty Christmas tree in his arms. His face was icy cold when he leaned over to give me a kiss. As he began to get warm, he told me how he had managed to get home. He and Nathan met a man with a truck headed out of Cambridge and asked if he was going their way.

"I'm only going as far as St. Michael's," he told them, "and you're welcome to ride along if you're willing to ride with a corpse."

"We don't care if it's the Devil himself," they told the man and climbed in the back of his truck. Sure enough, there was a corpse in the back. They rode all the way to St. Michael's with it sliding back and forth at every bump and turn. Apparently, the hearse couldn't get through the snow drifts and he agreed to take the body to St. Michael's. At St. Michael's, Bob and Nathan got a ride in another truck that brought them home to Tilghman.

"And here I am!" said Bob.

"I'm glad you're here, but I'm glad it wasn't me who had to ride with a corpse," I told him.

It was early morning before we finished trimming the tree. Bernard stayed to help put it up. We hadn't been asleep an hour when Reed and Angela came to jump all over the bed.

"Did Santa bring us a tree?" they shouted.

"Let's go see," we told them and together we all trooped downstairs. Bursting with excitement, they rushed to the tree and scooped up the toys I had made for them, a boy doll for Reed and a girl doll for Angela. Reed got a red wagon and Angela got a doll carriage. Their stockings were stuffed with fruit and nuts.

"Santa came!" they sang out in chorus. "We knew he would."

Watching their happy faces, I bowed my head and thanked God for answering my prayer.

The Marine Police were always in the harbor to inspect the oysters when the dredgers returned in the evening. They checked to be sure if the oysters were legal size or too small. The buy boats were there, too.

One evening Bob was buying oysters when the Marine Police came aboard to inspect his oysters. The police passed them as okay. Bob proceeded to sail to Cambridge to J. M.

Bramble's oyster house. Another policeman came aboard and arrested Bob for small oysters. They confiscated his boat and took him to Easton jail. Boy, was Bob furious! He told them that the oysters had already passed inspection; evidently they didn't believe him or didn't care. The jailkeeper whom Bob knew didn't put him in a jail cell. He thought it was ridiculous that the police had arrested him.

Bob called me and told me he was in jail. I was so thunderstruck I couldn't believe it.

When the jailkeeper heard him say he was in jail, he said, "You aren't in jail now, but you will be!" And with that, he locked him in a cell! I put the children in the truck and drove to Easton to bail him out.

His trial was set for the next month. In the meantime, the police shoveled his oysters overboard and wouldn't let him use his boat. Bob was so furious that he couldn't sleep. One night he was talking in his sleep. I heard him saying, "Yes sir, I am going to take all the oysters I can find and dump them on the Courthouse steps."

At his trial, Bob told the judge what had happened, but all he did was bang his gavel down, and exclaim, "Guilty as charged; you will pay a fine of $75."

If you think Bob was mad before, you should have seen him as he paid his fine and stamped out of the room. He drove home and swore he would never buy another oyster but, of course, he relented in time. I thought we would be disgraced forever, but it proved to be just another lesson in the course of our life together.

The Marine Police used him as a scapegoat for other watermen. Every once in a while they have to arrest someone. Bob just happened to be there at the wrong time.

21

Reed's Experience on Ice

In 1936, the Bay froze over and the dredge boats were frozen in the harbor. The men had to walk on the thick ice to keep their boats pumped out.

I guess Billy Sommers, Reed's older friend, thought he would try walking on the ice like the men. Reed tagged along with his sled.

I was down at the shore and didn't see them until they were too far out to hear me call them. My heart nearly stopped when suddenly one of them disappeared. I didn't know which one it was, then I saw Reed lie down on the ice and push the sled toward the hole. Billy grabbed it and used it to pull himself up on the ice. They gradually made their way back to shore and a warm fire. I didn't need to scold Reed. He was too frightened to try such a thing again.

The children had plenty of friends with whom to play and get into mischief. Glenna Kapisak and Angela tried everything. One day, they threw mud on Katherine and Ray Kapisak's porch and had to wash it off. Another day, they walked past the church and found the door open, so they decided to go inside. There, the money was still in the collection plates.

"We found some money," they said happily when they brought it home. They weren't so happy when I marched them back to the church to return it.

Two of her other friends were older, Dot Harrison and Ellen Ann, but they all played together just the same. It was a wonderful place to raise children. They had everything in a nutshell, freedom to play and neighbors to worry about them when they were sick. So many memories to keep.

Nor any ice to break. The Annapolis, reconditioned in the summer to meet conditions as severe as those in the winter of 1935-36, bobs with the tide at her President street pier, unused this season.

Boats frozen at Tilghman.

22

Blue Fish Incident

In the summertime, some of the watermen had purse nets which were spread out in the water. One boat takes all the nets, another boat takes a hold of the end of the net and when they see an oil spot or fish coming to the top of the water, they row all around the fish with the net, spreading out the net. There is a rope fastened to the bottom of the net. This is pulled into a purse-like shape to hold the fish. The fish start to jump and fight the net, but the fishermen are faster. The fish, mostly bluefish, are pulled in the boats with the net.

The men start making the purse nets in the winter. Blanche Bozman and I helped make them one winter. We used a fish net shuttle to catch the netting together. It is very fascinating to do, but your hands sure get real tired.

When the bluefish were plentiful, Bob looked around for a wider market. He found one in Wilmington, Delaware and arranged to take a load there twice a week.

He had made our Chevrolet car into a truck so he could haul the fish boxes. He also hired a young boy to help him.

Late one afternoon, Bob and the young boy started for Wilmington, his truck loaded with Bluefish. He expected to be home the following afternoon. This was one day the whole Island will never forget. At about eight o'clock at night, Myrtle came up to tell me I had a phone call from the hospital in Wilmington telling me that Bob was in a tractor trailer accident. I was cleaning up the dishes from supper but was so worried that I didn't wash another dish. The hospital reported that it would be a miracle if Bob recovered.

Captain Bain and Myrtle offered to take me to the hospital. We left dishes on the table and I started to dress the children. I didn't know how badly he was hurt. All I could think of was getting there. In my haste to dress Angela and make myself presentable, I lost track of Reed. I called and got no answer. I ran through the house searching every room. I found him in his room on his knees.

He looked up and said to me, "Mother, you have always taught us to pray."

I was so humbled by his words that I burst into tears and knelt down beside him to pray for his father. I was so upset that I hadn't taken the time to pray.

Soon we were in the car on our way to the hospital. The children were only allowed in the lobby so Myrtle stayed with them while Captain Bain and I were taken to Bob's room. All I could see were bandages; the only open places were for his eyes. He was unconscious. All I could do was sit there and hold his hand and try to talk to him.

Later the doctor came in and explained that he had a concussion from a blow on his head. He had a gash from his eyes all the way to the back of his head. which the doctor had sewn up. Now was the critical time with nothing to do but wait. Captain Bain and Myrtle took the children home and promised they would return the next day with some clothes for me. In the meantime, I had no place to stay. The doctor gave me permission to stay in Bob's room for the night; I was so grateful. If he regained consciousness, I wanted to be there. I sat with him all night; sometimes he would twist and turn like he was trying to get away from something, muttering words to himself. In the early hours of the morning, I dozed off to sleep. The nurse and doctor came in. He didn't give me much hope for his body was battered badly with broken ribs and internal injuries.

When the people of Fairbank found out about the accident, they all offered to help in any way they could. Mr. Walter Weber had a daughter living in Wilmington. He knew Bob would be in the hospital for quite a while, so he made arrangements for me to stay with his daughter. It was a very kind thought, but I wasn't going to leave the hospital until Bob was out of danger.

Sometime the next afternoon, he opened his eyes, but was not conscious. This frightened me, but the doctor reassured me that he was better and that a head injury confused your brain.

"He's a big strong man and if he has survived this long, I'm sure he'll make it." I gave a sigh of relief and hope sprang back into my heart. Another day passed before Bob was really back into the world, asking about his bluefish and if someone took them to market. That night, Madge took me to her house. She had a large family but was glad she could help me. She wanted me to stay as long as Bob was in the hospital. It was so wonderful to sit down and have the cup of hot tea and piece of cinnamon toast which she made for me. After a hot bath and a good night's sleep, I was ready to tackle the world the next morning. The hospital was a short distance away so I declined her offer for a ride and enjoyed the walk.

It was several days before Bob was up to talking. At last he told me what happened. He was sleepy and pulled off on the side of the road to take a nap as his lights were very low and he was afraid to drive. He was asleep when a tractor trailer sideswiped his car. When he came to, he was crawling on his hands and knees in the middle of the highway. The truck driver was standing over him with a revolver. Just then a highway patrol drove up. The truck driver disappeared into the darkness and the highway patrol took over. He called an ambulance for Bob, cleaned up the fish boxes which were all split open. Fish were all over the road. We never heard or saw the young boy again. Bob said he remembered someone trying to wake him up just before the trailer hit him. Anyway, I'm sure the boy was so scared that he jumped out and maybe is still running!

Bob was in the hospital for two weeks, then the doctor was so pleased with his recovery that he was allowed to leave for a few days. All the time Bob was in the hospital, the State Road Police stood outside his door. I was really furious, but Bob didn't know it was against the law to stop on the highway. Anyway, the day Bob was released from the hospital, he got a summons to court. I don't remember what the fine was but we were just glad to be going home. We thanked our friends for their kindness and went to the garage to see the damage of our car. What do you think we found? Just the chassis, steering wheel, motor and wheels. It seems impossible someone could live after seeing the car! Only the Lord knows and we were grateful. Bob told me later, when he first went to the hospital, he was partly conscious when the doctor was sewing him up, Bob heard him say, "I'm going to sew him up, but he'll never live." Maybe that was what Bob needed to make him fight harder.

A week after we returned home, Bob and Nathan Parks took the bus to Wilmington and drove the remains of the Chevrolet home. Everyone went out in the road to see the wreck, with Bob and Nathan sitting on the chassis.

We sold the motor and tires which weren't much. Bob lost his customers so he went back to crabbing for the rest of the summer.

23

Another Surprise

After our Chevrolet was mangled, we didn't have transportation. Bob looked for a used truck, but nothing seemed to be available. He wanted to retail fish and crabs again because he needed a second summer job beside crabbing in the summertime.

One day, he left early for Easton with Ruth Haddaway when he brought the mail. He didn't say where he was going. Sometime in the afternoon I heard the crunching of oyster shells in the driveway. Someone was driving a new truck! I went out to see who it was. Bob stuck his head out the window and called me. I was so stunned that I just looked at him.

"Whose truck do you have?" I inquired curiously.

He smiled and said, "It's ours, honey, isn't she a beauty?"

"But a brand new Ford!" I exclaimed. Then I looked at the door. He had his name, telephone number and "seafood" painted in fancy red and white letters. "You did this all in one day! It must have cost a fortune!" I marveled, looking puzzled.

"It was only nine hundred and fifty dollars," he smiled at me with his impish grin that he knew would melt my heart. Don't look so glum, I've never failed you yet, have I?"

"No, but you sure are full of surprises", I admitted. In looking back, I think this is what kept our marriage together. I trusted Bob completely and it always worked out one way or another. Bob could be so persuasive, I sometimes said he could sell a boat to a man out in the middle of the desert.

The next morning, after fishing the pound nets, he loaded up with fish and set off to the hotels and boarding houses. It proved to be a good business, and we never regretted buying the truck.

I let Reed, who was about five years old, go with him on some short trips. Angela was still a baby, but once in a while, we all went along just to get away from housework. We had a lot of fun that summer, stopping for picnics and sometimes treating ourselves to a movie.

One day, Reed and Bob went by themselves. In the evening when they returned, Reed was dressed in clothes two sizes too big for him.

"I wish I had a camera," I laughed. "Did someone steal your clothes?"

"It's not so funny, Mom", Reed started to talk, "I fell down a well."

"A well!" I gasped. "Where?"

"Now, honey, he's all right", Bob defended.

"Dad saved me", Reed proudly stated. "I went up to a lady's house and knocked on the door to ask if she needed any seafood. I backed away and fell all the way down a dark well under the water. I came up spitting. Dad was climbing down the well with his hands and feet sprawled on each side of the bricks. He told me to grab his feet, then he climbed backward up the well with me hanging on his foot. A man grabbed me and carried me into the house", Reed continued.

Bob looked at me. "What else could I do? There was no ladder so I had to go down and get him! These are all the clothes the lady had."

When I recovered from the shocking story of my son down a well, I hugged them both. "Well, young man, you've had quite a day. I think you and your dad are heroes, but from now on, you're staying home. Get those clothes off and take a hot bath. After a bowl of soup, you're off to bed."

It was some time before Reed begged to go again. When he did, I said, "Only on the condition that you let your father do the selling!"

Elementary Public School, Tilghman, Maryland, where Reed and Ann went to school.

Angela, Reed and our new truck.

24

Trip to Norfolk

When pound net fishing was over, there was no place to buy fish. Bob needed to keep his customers supplied. Now that we had a new truck, Bob drove all the way to Virginia and took the ferry to Norfolk where the ocean fishermen sold their fish. It took all day for the trip, but it was worth it. He stored the fish in Harrison's ice house at Tilghman to keep them fresh.

It was a good summer. Bob kept insisting that the children and I take a trip with him. I was glad to get away from the humdrum of housework. It was a beautiful drive in August when the fall flowers were in bloom. All along the highway in Virginia, the crepe myrtle trees bordered the road. I don't think I've ever seen such beautiful trees.

As we boarded the big ocean ferry, it began to rain, the rain coming down in sheets with the wind blowing a gale. This wasn't the Chesapeake Bay, it was the Ocean, some difference. I didn't think much of that, but like everything else in life, another new adventure ahead of me. I remember when we got out of the car and went inside, the radio was blaring out Burns and Allen. Everyone was sitting around listening to the jokes. Hearing laughter helped keep away that scary feeling of the bumpy ride we had that night. Everyone else didn't seem to mind the storm, but I was glad when the captain called "all ashore".

We found a nice place to stay for the night. There were no motels in those days, only big hotels and boarding houses. The next day the sun was out, and we were ready to explore the City after breakfast. We spent all day browsing through the different shops. I bought a few souvenirs and stopped for lunch at a dear little lunch shop. We bought the children a toy apiece then went back for dinner at the boarding house.

We had seen a beautiful church, so Sunday morning we dressed the children and walked to the church. It was big with cathedral ceilings and red velvet cushioned pews. It seemed so grand after our Little Chapel, yet somehow with all its grandeur, the pipe organ and choir couldn't replace the feeling of quiet solemnity of the Little Chapel.

It was a wonderful trip. The experience of the Ocean Ferry was my first and last. I will never forget the beautiful drive and the crepe myrtle trees or the city of Norfolk, Virginia.

Fall

The lazy days of summer are turned to fruited fall.
The harvest of the toiling hours is heaped from wall to wall.
The frost is on the meadow, and far above in the darkening night
The honking geese wing their way on their Southern flight.
Each season has its beauty, but Fall to me is best,
To sit by the crackling fire and hold your dreams to your breast.
The leaves lie deep and wet in piles of burnished gold,
The fuzzy caterpillar crawls within, and yet- behold-
Spring brings forth the butterfly in gold array
To tell us God makes all things beautiful in his own way.

25

Two More Blessings

In 1938 and 1939 the Lord blessed us with two more gifts. Alice Patrice came March 2, 1938, a happy baby with steel grey eyes like her Dad's, and a head full of curls.

My health had been great, then on the night Patti was born, I had another heart problem. Mother came to my rescue again, taking up the duties as housekeeper and grandmother. She loved babies and devoted herself to her job.

I remember Miss Annie Dobson coming in to see the new baby, Patti, making herself known by crying at the top of her lungs. Miss Annie put her thumb in her mouth, much to my disapproval, but it did wonders for Patti. From that day her thumb was her constant companion. Nobody could pry it out of her mouth.

She was almost a year old when she came down with bronchitis. Again Dr. Reeser demanded onion poultice and again our house was an onion factory, but I was much wiser now and knew the tricks.

Even before Patti could read, she toddled around with a book in her hand, begging for a story. Since Angela was seven years old, I had time to read and rock Patti to sleep.

I didn't know where her head of curls came from until Mother reminded me that her brother, Gene, had curls, which he hated when he became a man. I didn't have to spend hours winding cloth curlers on her head like I did Angela's. When Angela started school, her curls were too time consuming to brush, so I had it cut in a short bob with bangs. Mr. Thompson, the minister at St. John's, had a barber shop in Easton. I took Angela there for her haircut. I insisted on a last picture with her curls, and she dutifully climbed onto the chair to pose like a little lady.

I think I was more upset than she was for her first day of school. I made her a navy princess-style dress trimmed with red braid. I tried bound buttonholes for the first time. I'm sure they weren't perfect, but I thought so. Narrow white ruffled embroidery, just peeking below little girl's skirts, was in style. Of course her dress followed suit.

On November 2, 1939, Susanna Coral arrived amid one of the worst winter blizzards. The electric lines could not withstand the ferocity of wind and snow. They came crashing down and with them, our lights were gone; we were lost in darkness. I lit the lamps which I kept for emergencies. In a few minutes everything reminded me of our first days of housekeeping: a snug wood stove and kerosene lamp.

Sue still loves wood fires and coal oil lamps. I'm sure that somewhere in her brain, she remembers drawing her first breath of life under those wintry conditions,

The roads were almost impassable, but of course it didn't stop Dr. Reeser from his calls of birth or deathbeds of mercy. Susanna was a bundle of beautiful big brown eyes pushing through a crown of black hair. From the stormy night she was born, her crying rang through the house. We tried everything from rocking to walking the floor with her. Dr. Reeser suggested a specialist, but even he found nothing wrong.

When she was six months old, she threw her bottle on the floor and refused another. Dr. Reeser put her on Pablum (a baby food). It agreed with her as far as food, but the crying continued. The neighbors all rocked her but Sue was determined to cry.

Captain Bain was very ill so Bob spent the nights with him, but he always walked the floor with Sue first. One night, he walked the floor with her until she fell asleep. With a sigh of relief, he tucked her into bed and I fell asleep. I don't know how long I slept, but when I woke up, everything was so quiet. I couldn't believe she was still sleeping. I walked over to her crib to find her wound up in her blankets, not even her face showing. I threw the covers off to find Sue blue in the face, gasping for breath. I was so stunned that I could sleep through her crying. Quickly I grabbed her and called Dr. Reeser. I was sure she was dying. Dr. Reeser answered in a sleepy voice, "Throw her up in the air!"

In a moment, life was restored and she fell into a natural sleep. Why didn't I think of that? My legs were so wobbly I almost fell, so for the rest of the night I kept Sue in bed with me. I was afraid to put her back in her bed. Maybe that incident was what I needed to never complain about the house ringing with Sue's crying. To me, it was a blessing. I knew she was alive. Maybe crying is good for the soul because it made Sue into a wonderful person, always thinking of others. She has a heart of gold.

Alice Patricia Bradshaw

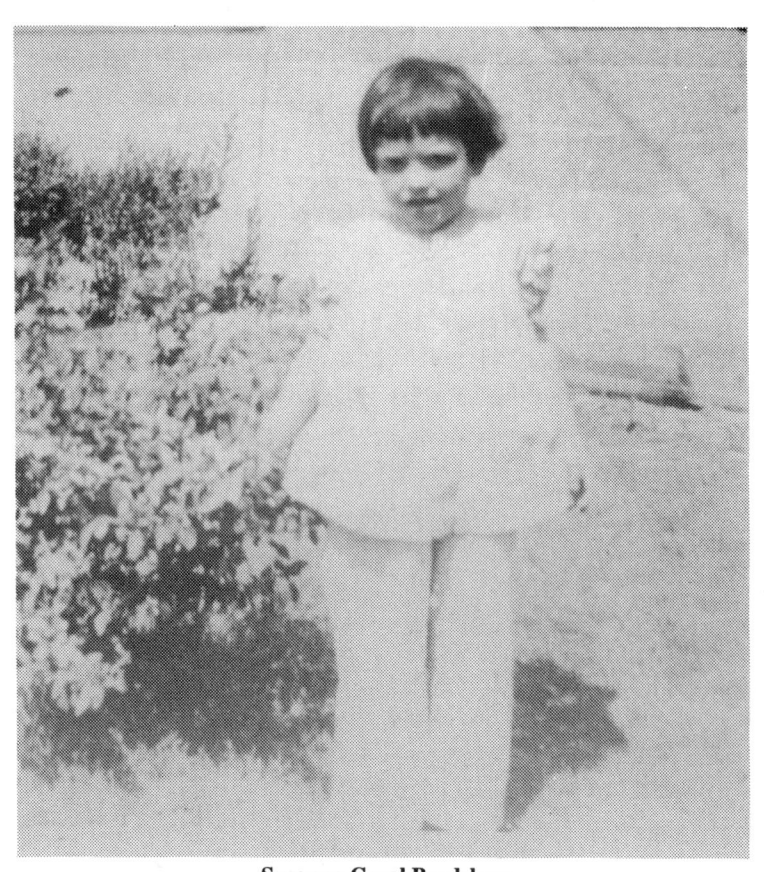

Susanna Coral Bradshaw

Sue - first grade

26

Fishing Parties

Fishing parties became a new line of business on the Island. City people were anxious to have a place for fun and relaxation, so they came to the Island to fish and crab. Bob, like most of the men, took fishing parties to supplement his variable income.

The Western Shore offered better fishing. The men left home for Chesapeake Beach and stayed for several days. Captain Earn Jenkins never went to the Western Shore with his parties. Miss Rose fed and boarded the people. The work was too much for her, so she asked me if I would help.

Bob's work meant that he was away most of the time. My health was much better and I was thankful to be able to earn a few dollars of my own to help with the family finances. Bob was making good money; so I could use my earnings for the house.

I needed a set of good dishes, so I thumbed through our old standby, the Sears Roebuck catalog. I found just what I wanted: a set of beautiful Noritake china, white with small blue flowers. I thought it would last the rest of my life. For twenty-five dollars, I bought a service for eight. When they arrived, I was almost afraid to touch them, they looked so fragile. I just looked at them every day. Since I had no china closet, I set the table in the parlor for company. Of course, I washed them every week whether we used them or not.

The first Sunday Bob was home, we had a big feast with our new china. I set the table with candles, flowers, and the new blue tablecloth Mother gave us.

We had Bob's family for Thanksgiving dinner. Bob had learned the art of slicing the turkey and serving it by then, although he never could understand why it had to be done in a certain way.

Bob and Reds McQuay bought a dredge boat that winter. He was happy to finally captain his own dredge boat. They did well the first two years, but the boat was old and he eventually sold it.

The first year he dredged, I wanted to buy him a wrist watch. I thought it would be better than a pocket watch. I saved my money all summer. On his birthday, I gave it to him. He was so pleased, but he didn't want to wear it to work.

"But honey, that's what I bought it for," I told him and buckled it on his arm. I was sure the leather strap would be perfect for work.

The next day when he came home from work he was glum.

"What's wrong? No oysters?" I asked.

"Oysters were fine," he said. "Guess I'm just tired."

I discovered the reason for his gloom when he went to wash his hands for dinner. His wrist was bare. No watch. When I asked about it, he reluctantly told me the sad story. The strap had broken and before he could catch it, the watch fell overboard. He was heartbroken. I didn't want to let him know how I had scrimped and saved to buy it, so I told him not to feel badly.

"The next one will have an iron clasp," I joked. I never found one, and it was many years before he owned another wrist watch. We concluded that pocket watches were the best way to tell time.

Twice while we lived in Fairbank the Bay froze over. It was hard on everyone. For weeks, the watermen had no work. We pulled our belts in and awaited the thaw. If we wanted fish, the men cut holes in the ice and dropped their baited lines through. Sometimes they caught a fish. Otherwise, we depended on our chickens and canned vegetables from our gardens.

That winter, Bob told me a story his father often told: the story of Joshua Thomas, one of the most famous preachers on Deal's Island. He became sick and couldn't eat. Everyone thought he was dying. Joshua told one of his friends that God wanted him to go out on the ice, cut a hole and bring him a fish. The friend did as Joshua asked. He brought back a fish for Joshua to eat and he soon recovered. He returned to preaching hellfire and brimstone, as they said years ago, during camp meetings.

When the Bay froze, the men in the lighthouse had no way to come ashore. If the ice broke the lighthouse loose, the men would die, so several of the strongest men decided to rescue them. Bob went along because he was young and strong. They tied a rope to each other and pulled a skiff behind as they walked out on the ice. If the ice broke, they could use the skiff to keep them out of the freezing water. They didn't think of themselves. All they knew was that their fellow men were in danger. They made it to the lighthouse without an incident and brought the keepers home.

Once again, the church was our one foundation, a place where we could go to pray and sing. The steeple was a pinnacle of faith pointing skyward as we waited below for God to keep us until the ice thawed and we could resume our normal life again.

I will never forget the day Jim Price, Minnie's husband, died. He was on his way home from the Western Shore. He tried to guide his boat into the wharf, leaning over as if in pain as he approached. The men standing on the wharf saw his boat slowly coming ashore. Someone grabbed the bow, pulled the boat in, and tied it fast to a post.

They carefully carried Jim home. He was nearly unconscious. He had suffered stomach pains ever since he left Chesapeake Beach where he'd had a fishing party. Instead of going to a doctor there, he headed home. Dr. Reeser was called and immediately sent Jim to the hospital in Easton where surgery was performed. A stomach ulcer had burst and peritonitis had set in and poisoned his whole body. He did not survive the surgery.

When he died, Minnie became the sole support of their two girls, Virginia and Janis. Spunky, happy, Minnie took life as it came and never complained. She soon found a job at Tilghman, but had no transportation. She walked the distance in order to keep her home and children. Captain Bain helped her but she was determined to be independent. Both her children finished high school. Virginia went to work and eventually married Charlie Alton from Easton. During the Korean War, Janis enlisted as a nurse. Minnie sold her home and lived with Virginia, but this didn't stop her from working. She also became a nurse, but continued living with Virginia and Charlie.

Island people act very independently, depending only upon themselves and the Lord to carry them through their hardships.

Friends and Family

Among our many friends was Miss Annie Dobson, Captain Jim Dobson's wife. Their children were all married and lived in Baltimore. She had the most beautiful lilacs. In the spring, you could smell the fragrance just walking down the road. I often stopped by as I walked past the house.

Miss Annie was always mothering our children and she always had a verse from the scripture to inspire me when my spirits were low. She must have been in her late seventies, but nothing short of rain or snow kept her from walking to church on Sundays or through the week during revival services. I remember her as one of the finest Christians I ever knew.

The Kapisaks had a large family of children. They were all grown and married. John and Miss Ella had one son, Donald. He was twelve when Miss Ella became pregnant with her second child. She was a wonderful neighbor and taught me a lot about Island life. She became very ill during her pregnancy. The weather was bitterly cold in January when she was so ill. The neighbors stayed with her all day putting bricks and hot water bottles on her feet, but nothing warmed her body. John took her to the hospital. The doctor had to perform a Caesarean section to deliver twins. Sadly, Miss Ella never regained consciousness.

Myrtle and Paul Kapisak took one twin, and Anna and Nathan Parks the other. Ella, the smaller twin, was never well and survived only a little while. The neighbors all helped taking turns caring for the baby at night. Anna and Nathan raised Ellen Ann as their own. She grew to be a fine lady like her mother.

John and Donald moved to his mother's home. When Donald was eighteen, he joined the Navy. While stationed at Norfolk, Virginia, he contracted spinal meningitis. A snow storm had grounded all planes. He died before his father could get to him. Donald was brought home with two honor guards. One of the guards was Lucy Presson's son, Norman, who had joined the

Navy with Donald. Donald was laid to rest beside his mother. It was one of the saddest funerals I ever attended.

It also saddened me to look across the road to see the Kapisak's empty house. Eventually Ray, John's brother, married Katherine Gowe from Tilghman. They bought John's house and we became friends. We worked side-by-side in the church. They had a daughter, Glenna, who was Angela's age, and they became playmates, always into mischief.

Ray ran oysters with Bob during one oyster season. Bob and Nathan Parks also ran oysters together. One night coming home in a storm, the mast broke. The boat wallowed in the swells as the crashing waves washed over it. They were sailing around Black Walnut Point, but could not keep her on course. One of them bailed out the water while the other took one of the long oars which they always kept on board. Between the two of them, they brought her into the harbor. It was a big joke between the two of them in later years.

Janie and Adam Kapisak had one son, Chester. He died as a young man from a brain tumor. Janie was another worker in the church. Anna and Nathan had one child, Betty. She and Ellen Ann grew up as sisters.

George Cummings, Sr. and his sister Julie lived next to Adam. His wife had been gone for some time. Bob told me he always stopped by their house coming from school. Aunt Julie, made ginger cookies and always offered them to the children. George, Jr. and Theresa, his wife, lived with George, Sr. I think they had five children. Theresa was a great neighbor, always helping.

Gorman, another of George Cummings' sons, and his wife Addie had three children: Florence, Gorman, and Ruth Ellen, Reed's playmate. They laughed and fought together. Addie and I were always chatting together in one house or the other. Addie's family were members of St. John's Church, as were her mother and father, Aunt Annie and Uncle Bill. Henry, their son, and Grace were also members. They had three children, Henry, Andy and Margaret Ann. Grace was another church worker. She was one of the last to keep the church going until her health broke down at ninety and she moved away from the Island. Bob and I often visited her after we moved to Annapolis. She welcomed visitors whatever time of day. She loved to cook and sew and fashioned beautiful quilts and crafts of every sort. Whatever time you were there, you had to eat before you left. She was greatly missed when she moved away because she was everyone's friend.

The Tylers and Fluhartys lived next to her. Miss Rose Tyler was a midwife and helped bring most of the babies of the community into the world in her younger years.

Mr. and Mrs. Walter Weber worked in the church. They were faithful churchgoers. Their children were all married and moved away, but one who died young of tuberculosis.

Mr. Clarence and Lil Harrison lived next to the Webers. They had two girls, Darlis and Kathleen. Miss Fannie Bozman was a constant church worker. She and Schilling lived with her family on the bend of the road next to the church. They had three children, Blanche, Carlton and Clifford.

Miss Laura played the organ. Frank and their son, Levi, were the only ones in Fairbank that ran a taxi service. Mr. and Mrs. Frank Fairbank lived in the community but owned a farm next to St. John's Church. Their children were all away but Hedge. Hedge and his wife Hope built a home next to John Kapisak. They had one girl, Dixie.

Captain and Miss Florence Somers lived next to John. They had three boys, Calwood, Roland, and Billy. Billy was the one that was always getting into trouble with Reed until Reed saved him from an icy grave.

The McQuays, Marie and Carrol, lived down the road from Minnie. They had two daughters, Erma and Kathleen. They both played guitars for the church service. Donald Kapisak also played a violin. We enjoyed having young people working in the church. Captain Glendy and Marie Larrimore also lived next to Nathan Parks. They had two boys, Leland and Stanley. Adrian and Minnie Harrison later moved next to the Fairbanks. Minnie still lives on the Island. They had one daughter, Dot, who was

Angela' age and they became playmates. Down from St. John's Church were the Harrisons, Captain Eddie and Miss Annie Harrison. Lucy and Bobby lived at home to help their mother. Lucy was a beautiful dressmaker. They had one son, Norman.

Members of St. John's that I knew from the Ladies Aid and attending services were Captain Levin and Miss Ida Harrison. Their son, Levin, founded the Chesapeake House which is one of the finest restaurants on Tilghman. Miss Rose George and Hattie Harrison were among the constant workers for St. John's, also Hannah Larrimore.

Two of the prettiest weddings in Fairbank were Mildred's and Myrtle's. Mildred met her husband, Harold Schneider at her dad's. He came down with a fishing party from Pennsylvania. They fell in love and were married the following June. It was very hard for a girl to go shopping for her gown and trousseau because of the distance to travel. Bob and I drove her to Cambridge where she picked out her clothes. She had a beautiful white satin floor-length gown. Invitations were sent out to the whole village. She chose Angela, who was three years old, for her flower girl. I made her a floor length pink dress of organdy and lace and tried to teach her how to strew the rose petals. I also made Josephine's dress, who was her maid of honor.

The church members arranged a bower of flowers at the altar. Miss Laura played the wedding march as Captain Bain escorted her up the aisle. The reception was at her home, where everyone helped with the refreshments. We all enjoyed store-bought ice cream and cake, which was rarely heard of on the Island and a beautiful wedding cake from North's Bakery at Easton.

Myrtle was married very young to Peck Granger. They had a son, Bain, nicknamed Sonny. She was divorced and came home to live until her second marriage to Carroll Newcombe in St. John's Church. Captain Bain also gave her a large wedding and reception. They moved to New Jersey where he worked for Dupont. Their son, Carroll Wesley, was born there.

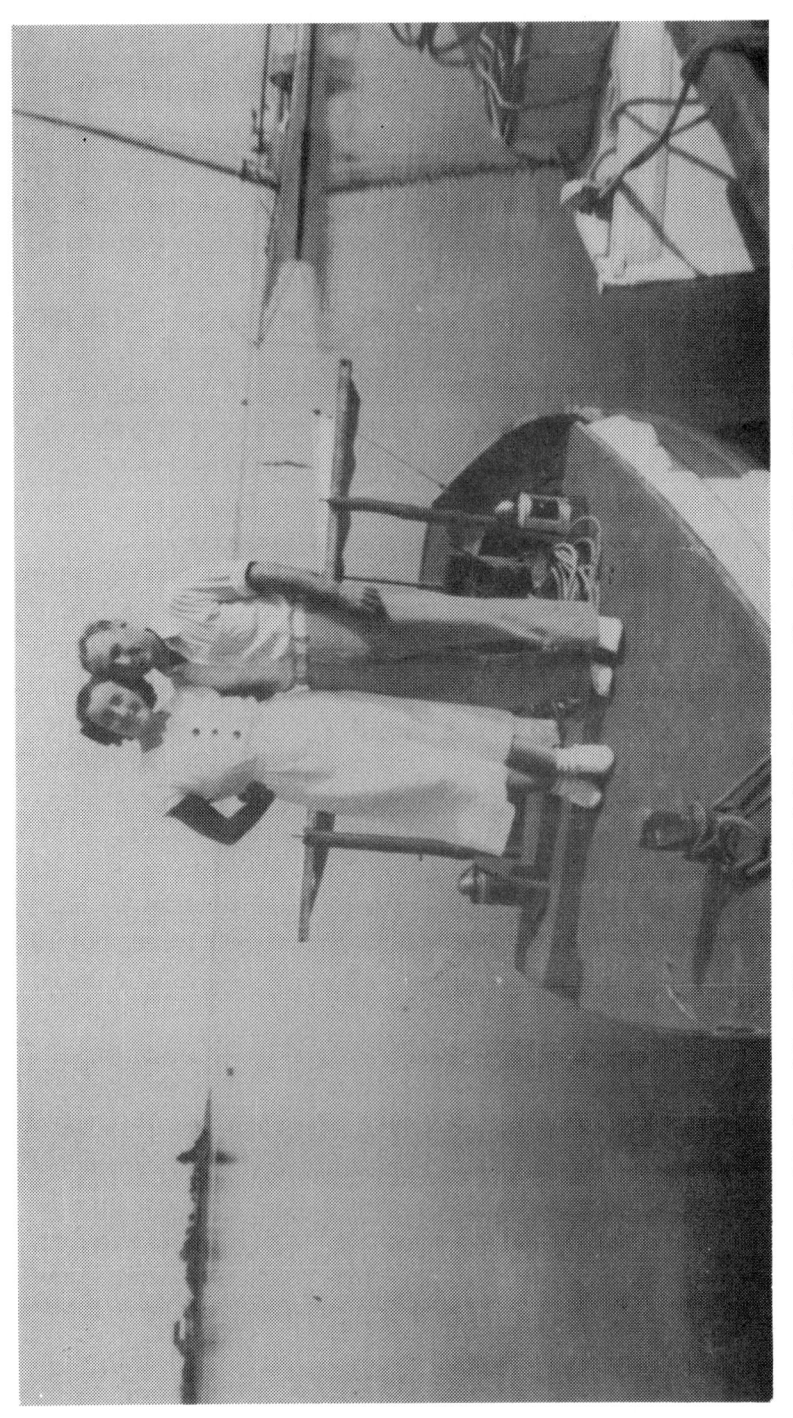

Myrtle and Carroll Newcomb, Black Walnut Cove. (Courtesy of Carroll Wesley Newcomb.)

Home of William (Uncle Bill) and Miss Annie Bradshaw - also later Grace and Henry's home.

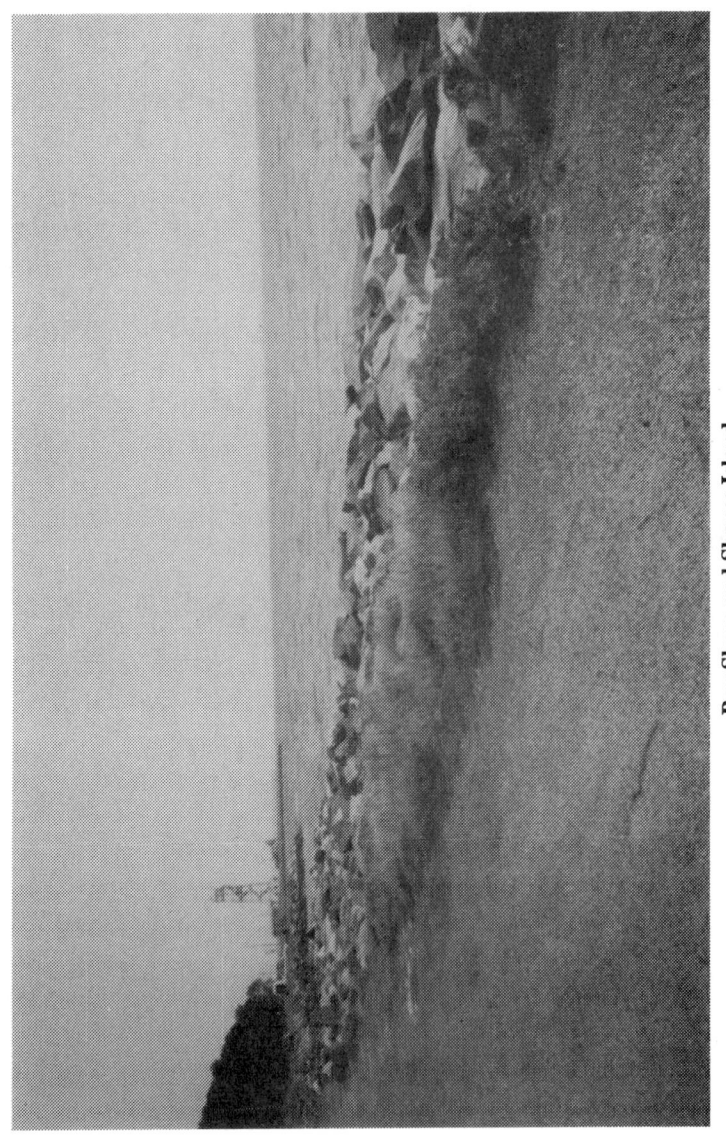

Bay Shore and Sharps Island.
(Courtesy of Gorman Cummings.)

27

Memories

Mr. Ruth, otherwise known as Rutherford Haddaway, owned the one movie house on the Island. It was upstairs above the firehouse at Tilghman. His bus took passengers back and forth on the Island and also to St. Michael's and Easton. On Saturday nights, everyone climbed on his bus, babies and all. No one had baby sitters unless their parents lived with them.

We enjoyed the comedies and good, wholesome movies which were featured. I long for the days when movies didn't embarrass the audience! I remember the pictures of the twenties and thirties when life seemed so much simpler. We thought that laughter really was the best medicine. It erased the tears of anxiety and fatigue of the week and kept us on an even keel.

Mr. Ruth also delivered mail to the Post Office at Tilghman and Fairbank. He ran errands and delivered medicine to those with no transportation, serving the people of the communities far beyond the regular duties of a mailman.

At Christmastime, he loaded his truck with packages. Nearly everyone ordered merchandise from Sears or Montgomery Ward. He never missed delivery even for a day, whatever the conditions. Many times he left his truck on the road, packed the mail over his shoulder and walked through the snow drifts until the snowplow could get through. Sometimes, the snow drifted so high over our doors that we were literally imprisoned inside until some of the neighbors came to shovel the snow away.

I remember our first radio, a gift from Minibel. We listened intently to the news, especially Lowell Thomas with his distinctive voice, describing far away events and places. We felt and saw all the tragedies and triumphs throughout the world, thanks to our radio. The children were allowed up to hear Amos and Andy,

Henry Aldrich, and Burns and Allen, then they were off to bed. We were never far behind. Watermen's lives began at dawn.

The fire house had only one truck. They didn't have any regular firemen. When there was a fire, the men of the community all helped. I remember only one fire in Fairbank.

Captain Bain's chimney caught on fire. The siren awakened the whole community at 4:00 a.m. Everyone was there in a matter of moments. It was a freezing cold night. The cold was worse than the fire. There wasn't enough fire to do much damage, only smoke.

It took days to clean up the water damage to the house. Soot and smoke ruined the walls. Everything had to be painted and papered throughout the rooms. There was one good thing about it; that was the year spring cleaning was done in the winter!

In 1930 we were overjoyed to have electricity! Our house was ablaze with lights. Reed kept turning them off and on every chance he got when I wasn't looking. I sadly put our Christmas candles away, packed up with my memories and treasures. We also bought a washing machine, gas not electric. No more wringing out by hand! The machine did it. No washboard to scrape my fingers now. Miss Rose wanted me to wash for her, she had so many sheets and tablecloths from her boarders. So I said yes, and the extra money helped pay for my machine. The tub was copper, larger than the ones today. It was Sears Roebuck, of course. My washday became much shorter. Life was really getting easier! No more coal oil lamp to clean, cut the wicks and fill; I must have gotten lazy with so many gadgets! Then of all joys, an electric iron; I didn't have to have the hot stove burning just to heat the iron. Everything was ironed, no synthetic material in those days to dry and fold. I usually had a clothes basket full of sprinkled rolled clothes to iron, with company coming in and talking in place of a blaring television. Reading at night was such a pleasure. I remember at home when we were all there. Nights found us all around the room with different books. If anyone found a funny chapter, it was read aloud for all to enjoy.

I remember so well when I had rheumatic fever and had to stay in bed. My bedroom was over the living room. Dad put a register over the stove to heat the bedroom. Mother always read to Dad while he mended a harness or cut shavings to start the fire.

Mark Twain was my favorite. I grew up with his tales of Tom Sawyer, the Indian cave and all the trouble he got into. I shivered and put my head under the covers, and finally slept, dreaming of skeletons.

My most embarrassing moment is still vivid in my mind. One time, I wanted to visit Mother and Minibel in Savage, Maryland, where Minibel was teaching school. I thought it would be nice to take the steamship which ran from Tilghman to Baltimore. It was a good time for me to take a trip because Bob was going up the Bay to buy oysters, and we would be alone. Mother hadn't seen Reed since he had pneumonia. I still had pangs of homesickness at times, especially in the winter when everyone was snowed in and we had to wait for the snowplow to clear the roads. Neighbors were always there to help in time of emergency. Bob always made arrangements for Clem, a man who lived by himself, to cut wood and shovel a path when he was gone.

This was our day to leave. I had dressed Reed in his coat, leggings and cap that I had just finished sewing the night before. Bob was heating up the car while I put on my coat. We were ready to walk out the door, when Bob popped his head in.

"Honey, we have a flat tire! You'll have to wait a few minutes," he said.

"Can I help? We don't have much time," I asked.

"No," he answered. "You'd just be in the way."

"Thanks alot," I said and slammed the door. The clock was ticking away. I was getting fidgety so I took Reed's coat off and checked to see I had everything. I looked again and my pocketbook was missing. I must have left it on the bed. I ran upstairs and sure enough, it was on the bed. I picked it up and ran downstairs, thinking I would really be in a jam if we had left before. I heard a thump and when I looked in the kitchen, there was Reed standing by the icebox with milk dripping all down his suit.

"Oh, no, what next?" I thought. "This sure isn't my day!"

I started scolding him while I stripped off his clothes and threw them in the sink. Big tears welled up in his eyes and that hurt look came over his face, just like his father's. I hugged him and said, "That's alright, son, I make mistakes too, just then I almost left my pocketbook."

Bob came in and said, "All's ready," then he looked at Reed and the floor.

"Uh oh, someone is in trouble," he surmised.

I glanced at the clock. We had only one half hour left.

"We'll never make it. I might as well stay home," I said with disappointment.

"Come on honey, don't be such a sourpuss. We'll be there, we can't disappoint the little fellow," said Bob. I cleaned up the floor while Bob dressed Reed and put on his coat and cap. Finally everybody was ready and I didn't forget my pocketbook this time.

The boat was just docking when we parked the car. Bob carried Reed and I picked up the luggage. We walked aboard. "Everything's okay, honey, we made it. I have to leave, the car is running," he said, and gave us a kiss. He walked down the gangplank.

Everyone was standing in line for their tickets. I set the luggage down and reached for my pocketbook. "Oh no, not again," I almost screamed as I saw Bob pull away. What would I do? I was the next in line for my ticket. I was afraid to look up and too embarrassed to look at the ticket salesman.

"Sir, I forgot my pocketbook," I said. With all those people, I could have dropped through the floor.

"Why, Mrs. Bradshaw," he said, "it is nice to have you aboard." Then I looked up. It was Mr. Chairs, Mrs. Dobson's son-in-law. Now I was more embarrassed than before, but he just smiled at me and asked me to step aside until he had finished with the other people. I took Reed's hand and stepped back, not knowing what my fate would be.

It seemed hours before everyone had bought their tickets and gone into the lobby. Then Mr. Chairs came over smiling again. "Don't worry about the money, I'll take care of it. Go to your stateroom and I'll take you home with Virgie and I." Virgie was his wife.

He summoned a steward to carry my luggage to my stateroom. I was so relieved I could have kissed him. I sat Reed on the bed and thought what a stupid fool I was to forget my pocketbook twice.

We arrived in Baltimore in the early morning. Mr. Chairs was there to take me ashore and drive me to his house. Virgie was glad to see me and welcomed us into her home. I called Bob. He had found my pocketbook and was wondering how I had fared without it. He made light of it by saying, "I was afraid you might have to wash dishes in the galley."

"It's not funny, I felt awful," I responded.

"I know," he sympathized. "I was just kidding."

Mr. Chairs put me on the bus and I received a check and mailed it to Mr. Chairs. It was a most embarrassing moment, but thank God for friends again.

One day, Bob went fishing and brought his fish home to clean and fry for dinner. I had gone to the store and when I walked in, Bob was stretched out on the floor, his face and hands covered with blood, his fish scattered over the floor. My first impulse was he had been murdered. I screamed so loud that everyone heard me and came running to my rescue. I knelt down beside him and tried to pull his head away from the stove where he fell. He was unconscious. I was so scared I could hardly move, but I pumped water onto a face cloth to wipe his face.

When he opened his eyes he murmured, "Good Lord, honey, what happened?" He was still groggy and tried to get up but he fell back down. Now I really was scared. I looked around and several neighbors were standing in the doorway.

"Call the doctor," I bellowed. Just then, Bob opened his eyes again. This time, with everyone's help, he managed to stand on his feet. He grinned at me.

"I was scaling the fish when I cut my hand," he said.

"Goodness, I thought you were dead! Don't ever scare me like that again!" I was still shaking in my boots. This was the second time he had fainted when he saw blood. Eventually I got used to it and never panicked again, but I ended up cleaning the fish and bandaging his hand.

Another time he had gone crabbing early in the morning. I was still asleep when I heard him call me. I jumped out of bed. He was standing in the yard, his face all covered with blood again. Then he fell flat on his face. I grabbed my robe and ran downstairs and out the door. This time I knew what to do. After I put cold water on his face, his eyes were open, but there was no grin this time. His mouth was split open.

"Honey, can't you ever stop bleeding, your clothes are a mess," I exclaimed.

He was in so much pain from his torn mouth I didn't know what to do. I wanted to call the doctor but he said that he would be alright. When he at last got in the house, he told me what happened. He was starting his engine when it backfired, the handle flew off and hit him in the mouth. I didn't want him to drive himself to the dentist but he insisted. By this time I had cleaned his face and he looked presentable. He drove off to Dr. Reeser instead of the dentist.

In about an hour, he came back staggering in the house and sat down.

"I told you not to go by yourself, but you are so stubborn," I told him. He smelled like a brewery. Bob never drank. I couldn't understand. Dr. Reeser gave him a glass of whiskey to numb his face so he could pull his teeth. Two of them were knocked out and two were loose. Another day in my adventurous life, what would happen next? I never knew, but living with Bob was an adventure in itself. We have laughed about these times and wondered how I ever put up with him. We decided that because he was so unpredictable, no one else would put up with him!

(Pictures on page 181 courtesy of Gorman Cummings.)

Josephine's High School graduation.

Another reunion - Bob, Mildred, Myrtle and Lloyd.

28

Captain Bain's Death

In 1938, Captain Bain's health began to fail. It seemed as though his spirit was broken and the friendly joking gleam was gone from his eyes. He still swapped stories with the men in Tom's store but his steps were slow and measured like an old man. I hadn't thought of him as old, only in his sixties, because he had always been such a vibrant man, eager to be up and doing. Bob noticed his decline and persuaded him to see Dr. Reeser who sent him to John Hopkins Hospital for further tests. They diagnosed prostate cancer. After surgery he came home, but Bob assumed all his work. Lloyd was married to Margaret Aikenhead, a girl at Upper Tilghman, as the people of Fairbank called it. They moved to Pennsville, New Jersey, where he worked for Dupont.

Josephine was the only one at home, She adored her dad. This was her chance to now take over the housekeeping and cooking which was a lot for a young girl of seventeen, but she loved to cook and clean, especially for her dad. I'm sure if her dad hadn't been sick, this would have been the happiest year of her life. Captain Bain never regained his health. Bob continued to take care of his boats, mend the nets and keep his boats in repair.

It wasn't easy for Bob because Sue was a very sick baby and many a night we rocked her crib and walked the floor to hush her muffled cries. At midnight, after he helped keeping her quiet, he spent the rest of the night with his father. It was another cold and snowy winter with drifts of snow so deep that cars couldn't make it. Captain Bain needed medicine from Jackson's Pharmacy at Tilghman. Since Reed was eleven, he offered to wade through the drifts for the medicine. Bob wasn't home that afternoon, so I let him go. He succeeded and with a sly grin on his face like his dad's, he said, "I made it, Mom!"

On February 24, 1940, Captain Bain passed away. He was remembered by everyone in the community as a man of honor and compassion for his fellow man. He was laid to rest in St. John's Cemetery with many of his loved ones. Wilbur, Bob's brother, could not come home because he was captain of a salvage ship at sea.

Josephine went to live with her sister, Beatrice, in Neavitt. Later she became a nurse in Baltimore and New York City. Bob fished his father's nets that spring. Then he repaired and painted his boats. Later everything was sold, except the G.A.C. Sailboat (George Albert Cummings) which was left to Bob. He was the only son working on the water, and it was his father's wish that he continue in this work. We also had the Lady Alice which Bob crabbed in all summer, but prices had dropped to almost nothing for crabs. Many people left the Island to work in shipyards, and Bethlehem Steel in Baltimore. The Kapisak boys who left for better money were among them.

The war was raging in Europe which called for more labor here. Bob put his carpentry skills to good use. Taught well by his father, he applied for a job at Fort Meade, and found work in no time. The children and I stayed on the Island while Bob found a place to board. Homes near Fort Meade were hard to find. When he came back and told me that he was making fifty dollars a day, I couldn't believe there would be so much money. I looked at him and said, "Honey, we'll be millionaires!"

"Not really," Bob slyly remarked, "but it sounds good."

Reed was twelve and kept the wood split for the home fires. He also nipped oysters in the fall. Nipping oysters is done with hand tongs. They are long handled shafts with small tongs to scrape up the oysters. The men stand on the boat and plunge the tongs to the bottom of the water. They keep pinching them together until the tongs are full of oysters. They are emptied on the boat and again the tongs were back in the water to refill. They were sunk back into the water to scrape up more oyster. The small ones were shoveled overboard to grow for another year.

If men were tongers, they learned it early in life and became very successful. There weren't many tongers in Fairbank, most of them had dredge boats. Bob never tonged. The process is even harder than dredging, but the oysters are usually better.

With his first money Reed wanted to do something for me so he went shopping with me to buy Sue a pair of shoes. I let him pay the clerk. When he gave him the money, the clerk smiled and said, "Sonny, you must be the man of the family."

"Yes, sir," Reed proudly remarked.

By mid December Bob was lucky enough to find us a house in St. Margaret's which is close to Annapolis. He paid the rent for one month. Then came packing time, what a job, which I did all by myself. It was a cold winter to be alone with the children, but I managed as always when things were tough. Mother's letters were more precious than ever. It was lonesome with so many people of the community gone, but always on Sundays was the Little Chapel and the companionship of friends. It seemed the bell was more welcome than ever. The air was crisp and clear and the bell resounded through the snow-laden trees like a benediction.

Bob didn't know much about his father's history because Captain Bain was raised by his uncle Jake. His mother died at his birth. They lived on Holland's Island which is located in the lower part of Chesapeake Bay. Through recent research Sue has discovered the Bradshaw family owned the Island in the 1700's. They sold all of the Island but their home in 1862. The Bradshaws continued to live on the Island until Captain Bain was a young man. He learned the art of the watermen and owned his own boat at the age of fourteen.

He married Mary Virginia Richardson in January 13, 1895. They raised four of their children on Holland Island. Bob was two years old when his father moved his family to Tilghman. Hollands Island was crumbling into the Bay. Caskets began floating away into the Bay. Most of the people moved their families from the cemetery to Deal's Island and Cambridge to preserve their bodies.

The rest of Bob's brothers and sisters were born on Tilghman. Ralph, Theresa and Luther died at an early age. Captain Bain was one of the best loved men of the Island. His pockets were always open to any need of his neighbors or strangers if they had no place to eat or sleep. The family attended St. John's Church. When Revivals came on the Island, he and his family were always there. He became so emotional at the tent meetings; he jumped so high his pocketwatch fell to the floor. He was joyful and kind to all. I enjoyed the stories he told of the watermen in the 1800's. He had such a way of weaving them into colorful tales.

Wilbur enlisted in the Navy during World War I. While he was still in the Navy, his ship "Killery" contracted with Merritt Chapman and Scott, a salvage company, to raise sunken ships. He spent the rest of his life in this work. After many years of study, he rose to Salvage Master, and Captain of his ship "Rescue". The "Killery" dry docted in New York Harbor, in New York City, once a year for repairs. This was the only time Wilbur came home. It was a rejoicing time for the whole family to have him home. He and Bob were great pals the short time they were together.

When he was not at sea his ship was based in Jamaica. He was a man of honor and high esteem among his shipmates. He made his home in Jamaica, where he met and married an English girl, Muriel Hilton, whose father was stationed there. They raised one son, Warren (Mike), who later became an aviator.

Captain Bain Bradshaw, Myrtle, Mildred, Josephine and Sonny.
(Courtesy of Phyllis Evans.)

Bradshaw family outing. (Courtesy of Carroll Wesley Newcomb.)

The "Rescue" (Courtesy of Mike Bradshaw.)

29

Leaving the Island

Two days before Christmas, everything was packed, furniture loaded, just waiting for the driver and family to step in and drive off. We had said our farewells to our neighbors the day before. It was hardest to say goodbye to Miss Rose. Now she had no one dependable to help with her boarders. I told her that maybe God would provide another special person.

"Alice, you are the best friend I ever had. Don't leave me." I turned my head, gave her a kiss and left. It really wasn't goodbye. Many times we returned and always visited everyone.

I took one last look and walked through the bare rooms. They seemed so large now that everything was gone. The varnish on the bare floors caught the light of the dying sun. I shivered, for now the house was cold. I wanted to feel the warmth of our family around the room again, the firelight gleam of the shadows against the wall.

The walls had gaping holes where the stove pipes had been pushed into the chimney. At that moment, I think I just realized the enormity of saying goodbye. In the back of my mind, I heard children running through the house, their giggles and squeals resounding through the thin cold air. Angela and Reed were playing in the snow with Mickey. Bob brought him home a tiny puppy. Now he was big and husky, part collie and part shepherd. Reed had trained him to carry the sled through snow banks with Angela hanging on for dear life. She tried it until the time he put her in the sled and Mickey took off over the frozen ice bound cove. Someone heard her screaming and stopped the dog. After that incident, he wasn't allowed to play with Mickey for a long time.

I peeked into the kitchen where Sue and Patti sat on the only two chairs left in the house. Always before, the kitchen at

Christmas was full of root beer smells sitting behind the store, and the aroma of fresh baked cakes permeated the air. Patti looked at me, big tears welled in her eyes. "Mommy how can Santa find us where we are going?"

I tried to hold the tears back. She spoke so seriously! I smiled and tied her bonnet. I wiped the tears away saying, "Well, honey, Santa is a wise old man who knows everything. Would you like to write him a note so he can find us?"

"Oh yes," she clapped her hands in glee. I pulled a piece of paper from my purse, gave her a pencil and helped her write her name and tell Santa where we were going. Now she was happy as we sang Jingle Bells. Sue joined in her baby voice. I sat her on my lap and buttoned her leggings. The car would be cold because this was a long time before heated cars.

I heard Bob's boots crunch on the crusted snow as he came in the door. "Time to go, honey." He picked Sue up and carried her to the car. Patti took my hand, still singing Jingle Bells. I closed the door, letting the screen slam. I thought of the times when I reprimanded the children, "Don't slam the door!" Now, anything was better than the silence of the falling snow.

The children were all snuggled in blankets with Mickey. The engine was running to heat the car when Bob slid behind the wheel. He smiled at me with his sly old grin, as much as to say, everything is going to be better. We passed the Little Chapel and I glanced at the steeple, which seemed to say "good bye" and "God Bless".

We boarded the ferry John M. Dennis at Claiborne and crossed the Bay to Annapolis. I thought of my mother when she left her home in Michigan to face the Wild West of Montana. We, like Mother, with faith in God and ourselves, accepted the challenge for a new and better life for us and our children.

John M. Dennis Ferry crossing the Chesapeake.

The Ferry dock at Claiborne with cars being unloaded from the ^Gov. Emerson C. Harrington, ^first of the Claiborne-Annapolis ferries, about 1915.

My Island Home

If, some day, you chance to wander
    Down on the eastern shore,
I'll show you the wondrous place
    Where I have lived before.
Some fifty years ago
    I came here as a bride
And learned the ways of Island Folks
    Where they lived and worked with pride.
Their homes were filled with love and laughter
    In good times and in bad
For the church was their one foundation
    And faith in God was all they had.
The church I love most dearly
    For there I found my way
And the quiet tree-lined church yard
    Where lie our dear ones of yesterday.
Each week the church bells call to worship
    The people on the isle.
Some come because it's Sunday.
    Others come to pray.
Each seeks to find an answer
    To make their lives worthwhile
                       Continued

For there's a certain something within its sacred walls
    That somehow holds the key
And gives them faith to find tomorrow
    And hope for all humanity.
The years have changed this Island home
    And many moved away.
Yet there is a yearning to shake the hands
    Of those we knew in yesterday.
Home coming is the time when fall is o'er the land.
    When the trees have turned to scarlet
Painted by the Master's hand.
    Here we renew our faith in God
And sing his praises loud and clear
    Until the air is filled with love
And we relive the days we held so dear.
    So if some day you chance to wander
Down on the eastern shore
    Find this place of rest
It will fill your heart with love and joy
    And God will do the rest.

Family Tree

Bradshaw Line

Andrew Jackson Bradshaw married Sarah Eleanor Price and begat John, William, Mary, Margaret, Hermit, Andrew, Jacob

Jacob Bain Bradshaw married Mary Virginia Richardson and begat Minnie, Wilbur, Luther, Beatrice, Robert, Theresa, Mildred, Ralph, Myrtle, Lloyd, Josephine

Robert Lee Bradshaw married Alice Geneva Butler and begat Robert, Angela, Alice, Susanna

Sheldon Line

Robert P. Sheldon married Susanna Kinzi McDowell and begat George, Charlie, Eugene, Jessie, Frank, Alice

Alice Rosetta Sheldon married Frank Sherman Butler and begat Ione, Floyd, Susanna, Jennie, Minnie, Reed, Alice

Alice Geneva Butler married Robert Lee Bradshaw and begat Robert, Angela, Alice, Susanna

Avalon a man-made island at Tilghman.
(Picture courtesy Gorman Cummings)

Epilogue

Today, the children are grown and have children of their own. Bob is gone, but his heart was always in the little town where we met. It was a time of hardship and plenty, but love conquered it all. I shall always be grateful that God placed me in this quiet community where love of home, family and friends came first. Time has changed the community. The neighborhood is no more as it was. If you drive through the streets it will seem like any little village of America. If you stop and ask questions, there are only four families left to tell the tale of a wonderful flourishing village of the 1920's.

My heart aches when I drive past the Little Chapel. It has been made into a home. The belfry and bell, which beckoned me to stay on my first visit, are no more. The echo of the bell is still on a Sunday afternoon. New people have moved into the homes where we laughed in happy times and visited the sick in time of death and sorrow.

I wrote this book to preserve for all time what was yesterday and now is gone.

The Sharp's Island Lighthouse has tipped to a forty-degree angle. Only time will tell if it will ever disappear. Few skipjacks dredge for oysters and the dredge boats no longer light up the cove. No longer do the watermen swap stories and wild tales in Tom Faulkner's store, spitting tobacco juice into the sawdust or the hot pot-bellied stove that sizzled and spat fire into the air.

The air no longer resounds with the sharp clang, clang of hammer against anvil in Adam Kapisak's blacksmith shop. The bellows blowing air into the red hot coals to heat the iron to form parts to repair a dredge or a plow is long gone to decay. Kapisak's store is gone too. Its shelves were filled with all the staples of food and supplies that furnished the necessities for their large family and those of their neighbors. Many of the homes are beautifully restored by strangers and will stand until the end of time.

Stanley Larrimore and his wife now own our property. He built a small bungalow, but has repaired his father's house and lives there. The last time I saw the bungalow, a 'For Sale' sign was stuck in the ground where our house once stood. As I passed by, I can still see the arbor over the kitchen door and the clematis in full bloom. The maple tree we planted for shade remains there, inviting small children to come and play under its spreading limbs, as our children once did. I used to lay a blanket down and sew while the children had make-believe tea parties for their dolls.

Captain Jim Dobson's house has been restored by his grandson, Wesley Chairs and his wife. They have kept many of his grandparents' treasures of furniture and items that really have no price tag, only sentimental value of memories of another day.

St. John's Church still stands ready to greet strangers who might pass that way. Only twice a year is it open now. The old bell in the steeple rings in the quiet air and echoes through the graveyard, a song of peace and good will to all men.

If some day you chance to pass that way, I hope you'll take the time to walk to the shore where Captain Bain's house with its large screened porch is mostly as it was, except today it is painted red. Once it was white with green trim and looked so inviting peeking through the tall shade trees which covered the grounds.

Try to picture Tilghman as I have told of it, a place to stop and gaze on the beauty and remember as I have written, a place to love and remember.

Bob and I had nearly sixty-one years of marriage. Many times, we returned to visit and worship in St. John's Church. Our children are my life now and fill my every need. I believe these little towns are what makes America great. In those that remain, their faith in God is a beacon of light for all men to follow.

The Call of the Chesapeake

Far out the night winds call me back
to the rolling waves of the Chesapeake.
Where the shadows of the setting sun
fall against the skipjacks in the cove.
The solitude of the waves breaking
against the hull, drifting with the tide
bring dreams of peace and joy.
A lone gull sits, its wings at rest,
and far above in the darkening sky,
the wild geese in one fell swoop,
gather in contentment for the night.
It calls me back to the salty air
of the marsh grasses along the shore;
To dig my feet in the wet sand,
and gather treasures from its depths,
calling, calling to be at rest once more.
A wondrous place the Chesapeake,
far from the noises and dazzle of city lights,
the soft bellowing of the sails bring
a yearning I cannot deny.
It brings me peace and my heart is blessed.

Alice B. Bradshaw

Appendix

Dredge Boats and Captains From Fairbank 1920- 1950

Bain Bradshaw	Cordie S.
William H. Bradshaw	Little Jenny
Gorman Cummings	Elisha
Earn Jenkins	Ruth
John Kapisak	E. C.Collier
Glendy Larrimore	Laura Barkley
Stanley Larrimore*	Lady Katie
Nathan Parks	Gladys Melba
Ed McQuay	Sadie Page
Roland McQuay	Reliance
Wood Summers	Willie Bennett
Walter Weber	Columbia

still working in 1995

The Eastern Shore of Maryland

The Eastern Shore of Maryland has always held an attraction to me, maybe because I spent some of the happiest years of my life there. To a child in their formative years, it leaves a speck and print on your heart.

It is a beautiful land of rivers, country roads, old Southern colonial homes mingled in with fields of tomatoes, cantaloupe, watermelon and peach trees, my favorite fruits and vegetables. Maybe because I was a farmer's daughter and grew to love the land. I had never seen such beautiful majestic magnolia trees with their fragrance floating through the air. It is a land of romance and old traditions from the 1600's. It was settled mostly by the English and Irish, a gentle people then and today. It is a vacation land of beaches and the lure of the Chesapeake. In 1916, our family traveled by train to Ocean City. Of all the entertainment, the merry-go-round was our favorite place to rest and have fun.

Until the Chesapeake Bay Bridge was completed in 1952 it was a place set apart from most of the world. Before the Bridge, ferries carried passengers and cars back and forth across the Chesapeake.

It was a long wait, usually two to three hours in the heat of summer or cold of winter. After you boarded the ferry, it was worth it. You could gaze out across the broad Chesapeake and see the white sailboats rising and falling through the white caps.

The restaurant served excellent meals of crabs, fish, clams and oysters. The Eastern Shore is noted for its mouth-watering seafood. Traffic became heavier each year. Everyone rushed to the beaches for sun and relaxation. Today there are two bridges going and coming from the West to the East Coast. In spite of the bridges, traffic is sometimes ten to fifteen miles waiting to cross the bridges on holidays or weekends.

Now when I cross over the Bay and smell the salt air and the marsh grass, I know once more that I am home. So y'all come, as they say, you will find it as fascinating as I did some seventy years ago. The food is the best you will find anywhere in the world. In all my years of living on the Shore, it has never lost its fascination. It is a quiet place of peace and tranquility.

The Wye Oak at Wye Mills, often called Maryland's state tree, nearly five hundred years old.

Butler family at Ocean City, 1916.

Alice and Allie Butler, 1916.

Dredge Boat Recipes

Baked Rock or Shad

1-4 or 5 lb. rock or shad
4 potatoes
2 onions
1/2 stick of margarine
1 lemon
parsley

Wash and salt fish inside. Place in an oiled deep baking pan. Cut potatoes in quarters and slice onions. Place both around fish. Melt margarine and pour over all. Place aluminum foil or lid over fish. Bake 350 degrees until fish flakes and vegetables are done. Garnish with lemon and parsley. Serves 4 or 5 people.

Corned Beef Stew

1 can corned beef
2 cups cubed raw potatoes
1 large onion
1 large can tomatoes

Place cubed potatoes, onions and tomatoes in large saucepan. Add water to cover. Cook until nearly done. Cut corned beef into small cubes and add to stew. Cook until done.

Corned Beef Hash

1 can corned beef
6 medium white potatoes
bacon drippings
1 or 2 onions

Cook potatoes until done, then mash. Cook onions in bacon drippings until tender. Add to potatoes and mix well. Crumble corned beef and add to potato mixture. This can be made into patties and fried, or put into a 2 inch high pan and baked in oven at 400 degrees until golden brown. Serves six people.

Oyster Patties

1 pint of oysters
1 cup cracker crumbs
1/2 t. seafood seasoning (such as Old Bay)
Vegetable oil for frying

Wash oysters until all grit is gone. Sprinkle with seafood seasoning. Place 1 T. crumbs in palm of hand and place two oysters on cracker crumbs. Add more cracker crumbs. Pat and roll together. Place on waxed paper. Heat oil (1/2 inch deep). Fry oysters until golden brown. Drain on paper towels. Serve hot.

Shortbread

2 cups flour
4 t. baking powder
1/4 t. salt
1/3 cup shortening (margarine or Crisco)
3/4 cup milk (more if needed to make dough easy to handle))

Mix first three ingredients. Cut in shortening until crumbly. Add milk, mix until all flour is mixed through. Place on floured bread board, knead until smooth. Roll out on board until 1/2 inch thick. Cut with biscuit cutter. Prick top with fork three times. Place on cookie sheet. Bake at 400 degrees until golden brown, about 10-15 minutes. Yield 12-14 biscuits. Variation: After mixing flour and milk, place in 2 inch high pan, smooth out and prick all over with fork. Bake at 400 degrees until golden brown.

Note: Bob worked this recipe out from the quantities used on the dredge boat.

Maryland Beaten Biscuits

2 pounds flour	1 cup cold water
8 ounces lard	Baking soda
1/2 t. salt	(size of a pea)

Work all ingredients together. Dough will be stiff. Beat 20 minutes with mallet. Pinch off in 3 inch balls. Pat down a little. Place on baking sheet. Prick with a fork Bake 400 degrees for 25 minutes.

Minnehaha Cake

Cake Recipe
1 cup butter
2 cups sugar
4 eggs, separated
3 cups all-purpose flour
1 T. baking powder
pinch of salt
1 cup milk
1 1/2 t. almond extract
Frosting (recipe follows)

Frosting Recipe
2 cups sugar
1 cup water
1/2 cup raisins
1/2 cup walnuts (broken)
1/2 cup dates (sugared morsels)
1/2 cup coconut
1/2 cup candied cherries
1/2 t. vanilla

Cream butter. Gradually add sugar, beating well. Add egg yolks, one at a time, beating well after each addition. Combine flour, baking powder and salt. Add to creamed mixture alternately with milk, beginning with and ending with flour mixture. Mix well after each addition. Stir in flavoring. Beat egg white (at room temperature) until stiff peaks form; fold into batter. Spoon batter into 3 greased and floured 8 inch round pans. Bake at 350 degrees for 45 minutes or until cake tests done. Cool in pans 10 minutes; remove layers from pans and let cool completely. Spread frosting between layers and on top and sides of cake.

For frosting, cook sugar and water until it forms a soft ball in cold water. Add vanilla and pour over fruit mix and spread between layers and on top of cake. Yield: 1-3 layer cake. Enjoy!

Fairbanks Crab Cakes

1 lb. lump crabmeat
1 egg, beaten
3 T. margarine
2 slices bread, crumbled

1 t. seafood seasoning
3 T. mayonnaise
1 t. mustard

Place bread in blender and blend until crumbs form. Mix all other ingredients in bowl, add bread crumbs and mix well. Form into patties. Put one-inch vegetable oil in skillet and heat until hot. Place cakes into oil and fry until golden, turn and fry other side until golden. Remove from pan and drain on paper towel.

Potato Salad

2 cups water	8 potatoes
1/2 cup sugar	1 onion, chopped
1 1/2 t. mustard	1 cup celery, chopped
1/2 t. salt	1 t. celery seed
1/2 cup vinegar	1 hard-boiled egg, optional
1/4 cup cornstarch	parsley for garnish

Peel potatoes and cut into cubes. Place in saucepan. Cover with water and add 1 t. salt. Cook until tender. Drain and cool. Mix 1 cup water, sugar, mustard, salt, vinegar and cornstarch. Stir until smooth. Boil other cup water and pour over vinegar mixture. Cook until thick and clear, about 3 minutes. Cool. Pour celery and onion on potatoes. Pour dressing over potatoes and mix. Add celery seed. Garnish with parsley and sliced egg.

Sweet Potato Pie

4 medium sweet potatoes	1 can evaporated milk
4 eggs (beaten)	1 stick margarine
1/2 t. salt	1 t. lemon extract
1/2 c. sugar	

Wash and cook potatoes until done. Cool, peel and mash. Add melted margarine, salt, eggs and milk into potatoes. Stir. Add lemon and mix together. Pour contents into uncooked pie shell. Bake at 350 degrees 45 minutes or until knife inserted into pie comes out clean. Yields 2 eight inch sweet potato pies.

Weather Sayings and Beliefs

The following selection of folk beliefs, sayings and their variations, collected from all over Maryland and surrounding areas, was drawn from the Maryland Folklore Archives, which are open to interested persons at the offices of the Maryland Arts Council.

Weather and Food

If you put corn in crab soup during a thunderstorm, the soup will turn sour.

Lightning makes milk turn sour.

If you finish all the food on your plate, there will be good weather tomorrow. (told to children)

Flora and Fauna as Weather Signs

Thunder is the sound of bread and potato wagons rolling.

The Moon as a Weather Sign

A ring around the moon in winter means snow.

Weather and Religious Beliefs

If a thunderstorm occurred right after a funeral, the dead person was presumed to have gone to heaven.

Happy is the bride that the sun shines on; Blessed is the corpse that the rain rains on.

Thunder is God dragging trunks around in his attic.

"Old Remedies of the Eastern Shore" By John Leagre

Not so many years ago, people used many different remedies to cure many different colds or coughs. You may laugh at these potions, but they were commonly used in this part of the county, the Eastern Shore.

For a nose bleed: tie a cold door key to the back of your neck.

To make a wart go away: Bury an onion in the ground. Remove it forty-eight hours later. Slice the onion and place it on the wart.

For a bad cough: Use one teaspoon of kerosene, a tablespoon of sugar in a small glass of lukewarm water.

For a nail in the foot: Tie a piece of fat meat around the foot to draw the poison out.

Hot Pot Cure for cold: Mix 1/2 glass of whiskey and 5 teaspoons of sugar in a glass and drink. Then go to bed immediately!

For a fever: Get a towel and wrap onions in it. Then wrap loosely around the person's chest to cure the fever.

To stop a baby's tooth from hurting: Hang a cat's tooth around the child's neck.

For a backache: Rub the back in garlic salt.

Jump Rope Songs of Children

Collected by Mary Helen, Sara and Julie Williams

School
Kindergarten (run through)
First grade (jump once)
Second grade (jump twice)
Etc.

California Oranges
California oranges, buy them by the pack
California oranges, tap me on the back

Skip the Ocean
Skip the ocean, 2 by 2
2 by 2, 2 by 2
Skip the ocean, 2 by 2
My fair lady

Superstitions

Do not paint a boat blue;
Do not carry black walnuts on a boat;
Do not carry fried chicken on a boat;
Do not turn a hatch cover upside down;
To buy wind, toss a penny overboard;
To buy more wind, toss more coins overboard.
When old sailors die, they return as seagulls.

Memories of St. John's Chapel

This church was our one foundation
    Each home found a blessing there.
We walked to church in dark and sunny weather
    When the bell rang its hour of prayer.

It was a time for gathering from the
    Toil of daily life.
Just to sit within its calm walls
    of peaceful fair.
We found strength to follow in God's
    footsteps and His care.

Happy times of laughter gave us courage
    In times of a loved one's passing,
And the promise of the life hereafter
    With God's love to share.

The ladies aid was an inspiration
    Where all could work and play.
Oyster suppers, festivals, and quilts to auction off;
    the preacher to pay.

Revivals came once a year to keep us
    When our spirits failed
to remind us God is still in power
    When we listened for the echo of the
    bell within the belfry tower.

Once more homecoming brings us
    to this house of rest
With love of friends and praises to
    Our King, may we be blest.

    --Alice B. Bradshaw, 2001